Such a Strange Lady

A JOAN KAHN BOOK

Such a Strange Lady

A BIOGRAPHY OF DOROTHY L. SAYERS

JANET HITCHMAN

HARPER & ROW, PUBLISHERS
NEW YORK, EVANSTON, SAN FRANCISCO, LONDON

This book was first published in England under the title *Such a Strange Lady: An Introduction to Dorothy L. Sayers (1893–1957)*.

The publishers and the author wish to thank the Estate of Dorothy L. Sayers and Victor Gollancz Ltd for their permission to reproduce extracts from Dorothy L. Sayers's books in this biography.

FIRST U.S. EDITION

Designed by G. Adelson.

Library of Congress Cataloging in Publication Data

Hitchman, Janet.
  Such a strange lady.

  "First published in England under the title Such a strange lady: an introduction to Dorothy L. Sayers (1893–1957)."
  "The works of Dorothy L. Sayers": p.
  1. Sayers, Dorothy Leigh, 1893–1957. I. Title.
PR6037.A95Z7 1975b   823'.9'12 [B]   75–6340
ISBN 0–06–011903–9

---

75 76 77 78 79 10 9 8 7 6 5 4 3 2 1

Contents

Illustrations

To Doreen Wallace

*with thanks for her boundless
kindness throughout many
years*

Introduction

When first asked by the publishers to write a life of Dorothy L. Sayers, I turned down the idea for several reasons. I was awestruck by the breadth of her work and did not think that, apart from the Wimsey books, I could possibly claim to interpret her writing. Then too, I knew that I could not have access to her most personal papers, and there did not at the time seem enough material at hand to make a book. In many ways Dorothy L. Sayers was a very private person, and some of her closest friends have declared that she "would hate to be written about so soon after her death." It was also said that she had laid down that no book should appear about her until she had been dead for fifty years.

It is now nearly eighteen years since she died. In recent years there has been a great revival of interest in her work, and consequently in her as a person. The question then arises, how far should one ignore the wishes of the dead? I would be inclined to say that their wishes should be respected, if one could be absolutely certain of what they were. I have read hundreds of Miss Sayers's letters, for she was probably the last of the great letter writers, and nowhere have I found it expressed that she was violently against a biography of herself—nor did she put it in her will. She was at times a hater of reporters, and frequently turned them rudely from her door; in spite of that there are many interviews with her in newspapers. It is true that in these interviews she gave very little of her innermost self away. One has to use her methods of detection to get at the "real" Dorothy

L. Sayers, and I make no claim to having done that.

This cannot be a definitive life of her. It is more like an introduction, but it is the first one. I have heard that at least two Americans are bringing out studies of her, as is a Swedish author and a German one, and through the years there will, doubtless, be many more. Although Miss Sayers would have been the last to admit that the public should always be given "what it wants," she did feel, as an entertainer, that the public merited consideration. She never entirely lost interest in Lord Peter Wimsey, though she did get a little tired of him, and felt he held her back from doing, not so much more important things, but things that interested her more. Nevertheless, she liked to keep an eye on him, and seldom refused permission for reprints and broadcasts of the Wimsey stories. Recently, due to the productions of the books on television, many people have demanded to know more of the creator of this "sprig of nobility," and I do not feel that her ghost will be troubled by meeting this demand with the material I have been able to uncover. What would have pleased her is the fact that there is almost as much interest in her religious writings as in her detective stories, and her translations of Dante are still being reprinted almost yearly.

I did not ever meet Miss Sayers, but I feel that I have known her all my life. Almost everyone I have spoken to who did know her, or worked for her, has at some time in the conversation said, "She was—such a strange lady." Always a "lady"—scarcely anyone referred to her as a "woman," even those (and there were quite a few) who did not like her. I have tried to discover wherein lay this strangeness and hope I have succeeded, if only in pointing the way for others who, in the years to come, may have access to the information denied to me. A great deal must be supposition, a reading between the lines of her published work. Here the student is fortunate, for no one put more of herself into her writing than did Dorothy L. Sayers. Where I have mentioned an actual fact, this has been verified, but minor mistakes may unwittingly have been made; all opinions are my own unless attributed elsewhere. I must absolve from any errors Miss Sayers's family, close friends and executors, from whom I had no assistance whatsoever. In some areas I met positive obstruction, on the grounds, presumably, that a book of this kind would be in "bad taste"—an assumption which, I do not doubt, would have caused my subject to burst into one of her frequent gales of laughter. Whatever she saw herself as, it was certainly not as an object of veneration.

Many people have written to me sharing anecdotes and sidelights on Miss Sayers, and to all of them I am most grateful. In one or two cases, because the person actually knew Miss Sayers and I did not, I have used their contributions verbatim rather than transcribing them.

Especial thanks are due:

To Dr. Barbara Reynolds, for her great help with the Dante section; to Dr. Howard Gotlieb of Boston University Libraries, for his unflagging efforts on my behalf in the United States; to Caroline Roaf and Lady Anne de Villiers, who assisted me with research in Somerville College and Oxford; to Mr. C. W. Scott-Giles, O.B.E., Fitzalan Herald Extraordinary, for the Wimsey heraldry; to Miss Mary Hodgson and her colleagues at the B.B.C. Written Archives at Caversham; to the B.B.C., for allowing me facilities for research, and to quote from their files; to Livia Gollancz and to Penguin Books, for allowing me to examine their files; to Miss Joyce Allingham, for allowing me to quote from Margery Allingham's introduction to her Allingham omnibus; to Miss Kathleen Richards, Miss Sayers's last secretary, Mr. R. A. Bevan, late of Benson's, Mr. Butcher of Reckitt and Colman, and Harvard University Library; and to Margery Vosper, Val Gielgud, Harald Melvill, Mrs. Bedford, Mrs. Rawlings, Miss Sanders and Eric Whelpton, as well as to many others for their memories.

I am very grateful to the East Anglian Arts Association for a grant towards the research costs of this book.

Finally, I must thank my daughter Rachael, who introduced me to Lord Peter Wimsey, who manages to carry all the plots and characters of the stories in her head, and who has helped me to avoid too many errors in this respect.

1

Wimsey Lives!

> She laid both hands upon the fronts of his gown, looking into
> his face while she searched for the word that should carry
> her over the last difficult breach.
>   It was he who found it for her. With a gesture of submis-
> sion he bared his head and stood gravely, the square cap
> dangling in his hand.
>   *"Placetne, magistra?"*
>   *"Placet."*
>
> Dorothy L. Sayers, Gaudy Night

Oxford in the height of the tourist season puts a great strain, not
only on the city fathers, but also on the wives of the young dons.
It is upon them, with their health unimpaired and their enthusiasm not, as yet, dimmed, that the job of entertaining many of
the overseas visitors falls. They can be seen on most summer
afternoons shepherding small groups of Japanese professors,
American psychiatrists, African economists or Indian medical
men in and out of the Bodleian Library, up and down the High
Street, giving intelligent answers to intelligent questions and
expertly steering their charges away from the larger groups—
associations of everything it is possible to associate, with their
fast-talking professional guides.

Normally it was a chore Catherine enjoyed, for she loved

Oxford, and love is nothing unless shared. But this afternoon was different. The college had produced a middle-aged married couple, white South Africans from Johannesburg. They did not seem to be at all academic. She could not find out whom they were attached to. Parents of a Rhodes Scholar? Important beneficiaries? A couple the Warden of the college had met on his travels, and gaily asked to look him up if ever they came his way? Whoever they were, they were not entranced with Oxford. The streets were so narrow, the buildings so low—compared with Jo-burg it was a *kraal.* They were unimpressed by the Bodleian; the Radcliffe Camera was not what they had expected. Christchurch was "pretty," the glorious vaulting of the Cathedral Choir "a bit too fancy." Nothing brought forth a spark of enthusiasm. "Well, Hetty," the man said after every stage, "we've seen *that,*" and mentally ticked it off. Catherine racked her brains for stories of scholars and martyrs; even the rakes were dragged out. A polite "Oh yes" was all she received in return.

The hot afternoon was a dreary failure, and it was still too early to suggest tea. Seeking some shade and relief from the traffic noise, she led them off Catte Street into New College Lane, thinking she would show them Magdalen College and the river. As they passed under the bridge she said casually, "This is where Lord Peter Wimsey and Harriet Vane became engaged." It was as if an electrical charge had entered the couple. Enthusiasm so lacking about reality bubbled over when the fictional pair was mentioned.

"After the concert!" exclaimed the woman.

"Yes," cried the man. "And that Mr. Proctor caught them at it."

"Not Mr. Proctor," said Catherine gently. "A Proctor, a sort of college policeman."

But they were not really listening. They were gazing in awe at the blackened stones of the bridge, murmuring reverentially, "So this is the very place."

Now they had to see everything, even if it meant going back to scenes already visited. And so they went to Balliol, where in 1912 Lord Peter Wimsey graduated with First Class Honors in the School of Modern History; to the Scottish Baronial excrescences of Alfred Waterhouse, which were adjudged "so right" for such a noble personage; and to Somerville College, the original of Shrewsbury College in *Gaudy Night*, Harriet Vane's alma mater, which also received enthusiastic attention. Now and again Catherine felt constrained to murmur, "But they were not *real*, you know—just people in books." But to this couple the only real things about Oxford *were* Peter Wimsey and Harriet Vane.

More real perhaps than their creator, whose memorial tablet in Somerville Chapel received perfunctory attention—Dorothy Leigh Sayers.

2

Dorothy—Early Days
to School Days

... What greater fame hast thou,
... than if thou'dst died
Ere thou wast done with gee-gee and bow-bow.
                Dante's *Purgatory*, translated by Dorothy L. Sayers

Oxford, in 1893, was much the same as it had been for over a
century. The railway had come, it is true, but the station, disguised as a castle, was safely out of sight on the edge of the city.
The main streets were laid with stone setts, and must have been
extremely noisy with the clop of horses' hooves and the rumble
of iron shod tires. Public transport was by horse-drawn trolley
and, what with its noise and the continual tramp of feet, Oxford
was certainly not a haven of rest, except within the college
quadrangles. If you were rich enough you could pay to have
straw or tan bark laid outside your house. Many of the back
streets had no surfacing at all and were a whirl of dust in summer and ankle-deep in mud during the winter. The country was
still very much part of the town and the river was its heart. Max
Beerbohm was at Merton College, C. B. Fry at Wadham and

Hilaire Belloc at Balliol. In this city on June 13, 1893, Helen Mary Sayers presented her husband, the Reverend Henry Sayers, with a daughter, whom they called Dorothy Leigh. Leigh was Mrs. Sayers's maiden name, and she was a grand-niece of Percival Leigh, one of the founders of *Punch* and a well-known amateur actor of his day. In after years nothing was to annoy Miss Sayers more than to have the "L" left out of her name; it was one of the few things about which she had no sense of humor. Dorothy means "a gift from God," and so she was to parents no longer youthful.

The Reverend Henry Sayers was a classical scholar and a fine musician. He had been educated at Magdalen College and at the time of his daughter's birth was headmaster of Christchurch Cathedral Choir School. By 1897 their house in Brewer Street was uncomfortably cramped, with father, mother, grandmother, maiden aunt, maiden aunt's parrot, and a boisterous, four-and-a-half-year-old, precociously intelligent child. She was so *noisy*. When she lifted up her voice, no matter if she was pleased or in one of her rages, the whole neighborhood knew about it.

It was decided that the best thing to do was to move to the country, but why it had to be into the bleak Fens is difficult to understand. It is true that the living was good, worth £1500 a year, a vast sum for a country clergyman in those days. The Reverend Henry had several people completely dependent upon him, including two maiden sisters and his elderly mother, and a brother, crippled by a stroke, who also needed occasional help. Mrs. Sayers had a small income of her own, but the Reverend Henry was not a lover of money for its own sake, although the way he interpreted the Christian Gospel called for quite a lot of it. Any lost or lonely creature aroused his compassion and sent his hand directly to his pocket. He was a High Tory in politics and found it somewhat difficult to explain the purchase of a bust of Gladstone, a Liberal, at an auction sale.

"Poor little thing, no one else made a bid for it, and it had to have a home," he told his family.

It was on a mild January day in 1897, with father and mother already installed, that Dorothy arrived at Bluntisham Rectory. She was accompanied by her nurse and Aunt Maud, who had carried on her lap, throughout the cross-country journey from Oxford, a particularly truculent parrot in a cage. Dorothy was wearing her best brown pelisse and a bonnet trimmed with feathers. As the carriage turned into the drive she cried out in astonishment, "Look, Auntie, look! The ground is all yellow, like the sun."

This sudden splash of gold remained in her memory all her life. The ground was carpeted with early flowering aconites. Later her father told her the legend that these flowers grew in England only where Roman soldiers had shed their blood; Bluntisham contains the outworks of a Roman camp. So as early as this and as young as she was, her imagination was caught by ancient Rome.

After Brewer Street, Bluntisham Rectory was enormous, and quite typical of the decaying barracks in which country clergymen were expected to live. In Oxford there was gas light and running water, even a bathroom, but here there were only oil lamps and candles which accentuated dark corners and threw strange shadows. Bathing was to be in front of the nursery fire in a tin bath, the water hauled up the back stairs from the kitchen by the nursery maid, and of course, hauled down again when little Miss Dorothy had finished splashing about and blowing soap bubbles. The rectory had a large square central portion with a Georgian façade and porch, and an ivy-covered wing on each side. It was framed by huge ancient trees which reminded the growing child of Tennyson's "immemorial elms"—though most of them were beeches. Nature study was not her strong point. The front of the house faced a rolling lawn, and beyond that the open countryside. The difficulties of running such a

Bluntisham rectory, Huntingdonshire, Dorothy L. Sayers's childhood home

place, of keeping servants, of getting tradesmen to deliver down the long driveway, were no concern of Dorothy's. Here, surrounded by loving parents, a doting aunt and adoring servants, the boisterous squint-eyed child could grow. Cousins came for the holidays and the "nicest" type of village child was allowed in to play. She could never have been a lonely child. The gardener's son Percy taught her to ride a black pony, showed her birds' nests and introduced her to a few naughty words. In the winter he taught her to Fen-skate, which is a bit different from ordinary ice-skating. She was always something of a little madam, spoiled but not over-indulged. No one could call her pretty, but she was certainly attractive, with her round face "jes' like a little dumplin' " as the villagers said, a deep dimple in either cheek, bright blue eyes and straight black hair cut in the pudding-basin style and no nonsense with curl papers. Later on glasses would correct the squint, but it was not bad enough in early childhood to make her self-conscious.

The Reverend Henry Sayers had spent a great deal of his working life teaching boys, but there is no evidence that he ever regretted that his only child was a girl. He educated her in the only way he knew—as he would have done a boy. She could never remember learning to read, so she must have come to books very early, but she was never over-crammed with knowledge. There were holidays by the sea with her nurse, and it was on one of those that she recalled, "the astounding moment when the realisation broke in upon my infant mind that every other person in the world was 'I' to himself or herself, as I was I to myself. I was being convoyed along the promenade at the time and I immediately communicated the startling intelligence to my escort. I do not think they were impressed."

This sudden awareness of one's uniqueness, and the uniqueness of every other living person, strikes most small children, as does the question "Why am I, I—and not Harry or Joan?," but most of us tend to forget the discovery as we grow older. Dorothy never did.

One day when she was six, her father entered the nursery carrying a shabby copy of Dr. William Smith's *Principia*. "I think, my dear, that you are now old enough to learn Latin," he said.

Recalling the event in 1952 in a lecture given to a summer school run by the Association for the Reform of Latin Teaching, Dorothy said, "I was by no means unwilling, because it seemed to me that it would be a very fine thing to learn Latin, and would place me in a position of superiority to my mother, my aunt and my nurse—though not to my paternal grandmother, who was an old lady of parts, and had at least a nodding acquaintance with the language."

Dorothy found committing Latin exercises to memory no more difficult, and quite as enjoyable, as learning nursery rhymes. She would rush to the kitchen to show off her prowess to the cook and kitchen maids; but though they would pronounce her a "caution," it is doubtful she amazed them. Folklore and mumbo jumbo were still strong in the Fens and no matter what classical nonsense she yelled to Percy, he could reply with gibberish going back to pagan times. The urge to show off developed early in the child, encouraged as she was by adoring elders. Before she was thirteen a French governess had supplanted the nurse, and three other girls were brought in to share lessons with her. The Reverend Henry Sayers was never averse to earning a little extra where he could. He took pupils for Latin, boys needing coaching to get into boarding schools, and the occasional youth cramming for the diplomatic exam, and he also gave music lessons. The rectory must have resembled in some measure a modern commune. Grandmother and aunt had their own rooms and special maids. Mrs. Sayers had her "den," Mr. Sayers his study, big enough for him to stride up and down and practice his sermons. Then there were the

Dorothy L. Sayers, aged nine

pupils, visiting clergy, the uncle, so sadly disfigured by a stroke, and his children, the governess, three living-in maids, the cook, daily women servants, gardener and stable boy. It must have been impossible for anyone to be lonely or to keep any secrets in such an environment. It may have been this "open living" in childhood that made her so jealous of her privacy in later life.

By the time she was fifteen Dorothy was fluent in French, which she spoke with as much ease as she did English, competent in German, and thoroughly grounded in Latin. Already she had learned as much as the governess and her father could teach her. She had read every book in the house, as well as the novelettes and adventure stories borrowed from the servants. From somewhere she had collected a supply of westerns and "Dead-Eye Dick" stories, as well as the school stories of the time —mostly, of course, boys' school stories. For most girls the early teens are restless times. Things are happening which are difficult to understand. It was not the custom in the early years of this century to discuss such matters with adults, even with nearest relations; and never, never with the servants. In that household Dorothy was closest to her father, but he, poor man, knew only about holiness, scholarship and music. The tears and tantrums of a young girl who was so much loved and indulged were beyond his comprehension. The majority of fifteen-year-old girls were earning their living, too busy for adolescent miseries. The very rich were concerned with their place in society, others were at school. School! Boarding school, that surely was the answer. Dorothy welcomed any opportunity to get away from Bluntisham, where she knew everyone—and they were so dull. She never liked the Fen country, which to her was interesting only when it was sinister and frightening.

No one who has experienced a "Fen drown" can ever forget it. The steel-sharp, high-pitched wind "calls out the waters," which then roar thundering over the land. Afterwards comes the silence, broken only by the slap-slap of water against walls and the crying of animals stranded on dike walls. Gradually the flat-bottomed boats would appear, rescuing cows, horses, and chickens. People were lifted from rooftops and brought to the church and rectory to dry out and be fed. Only when the waters "went home" was the real horror manifest. The bloated carcasses, legs sticking almost comically in the air, blocked gates and droves. Occasionally a dike man would be swept away, or a baby would slip off the roof to die in the water before help arrived. In the days before radio, television or even a widespread telephone service, Fen men had to cope with their "drowns" as best they could, and the great high Fen churches were built that way as much for the physical rescue of man as for the glory of God and the salvation of souls. Almost as bad as a Fen "drown" was a Fen "blow," when the wind whipped over the land, gathering up the loose, soot-black topsoil, roots and all, and whirled it three parishes away, dropping it in a great fog over Downham Market and Ely.

These things were not adventures to a sensitive child, they were nasty threatening realities. They stayed in Dorothy's mind until she exorcised them in *The Nine Tailors* many years later. She was never able to understand the Fen people. They were taciturn, and when they did speak, their language was incomprehensible. They had strange customs, were capable of barbaric cruelties and their humor was very black indeed. There was a game the boys used to play with live sparrows which particularly horrified her. When she reported one to his parents he was lugged by his ear to the door to apologize to "Miss Dorothy."

"That were only old sparrers," he protested. "They aren't good for nothing."

"God made them," retorted the clergyman's daughter, "so they must be good for something."

All very pious of course, and what did she know of the Fen farmer's struggle, where every element and creature was against him? The more she saw of this primitive world, the more unsettled she became. So, in 1909, with a head full of fictional ideas of a boarding school, Dorothy arrived at Godolphin School in Salisbury. She was sixteen, wore glasses and was tall for her age, with a long neck which earned her the nickname of "Swan" or, worse still, "Swanny." She came at the wrong time of the year, in the spring term, when the other girls were already settled in, and friendships made. And, because of her almost complete lack of learning in any kind of mathematics, she was put in classes with girls considerably younger than herself.

As boarding schools went in the early part of the century, Godolphin was a fairly enlightened establishment. Girls were allowed a good deal of freedom, the food was edible, and the headmistress, Miss Douglas, was kind and understanding. But Dorothy, who had been so anxious to get there that she could not wait until the autumn term, soon began to loathe the place. Although she was well ahead of her contemporaries in English and foreign languages, she was in other ways very immature. She had no interest in the things that occupied burgeoning womanhood—hair styles, clothes, parties and (giggle-giggle) *boys*.

Her first essay in print appears to be a review of the kindergarten plays in the school magazine of the summer of 1909. The plays were *Cock Robin and Jenny Wren* followed by scenes from the "dear old story of King Arthur." She was most generous to the infants: "All the actors were excellent, without a single exception." Tautology was to trip her up from time to time throughout her writing career.

By the autumn term she had jumped to the top classes of the school and had gained a full higher certificate with distinction in English. The following year she played the violin in the school orchestra, and took the part of Princess Graciosa in the *Ten Dancing Princesses*. She gained distinctions in French and

German in the higher certificate, and continued to contribute to the school magazine. Several of her essays were in French, of a very good advanced-level standard according to a present-day professor. She also produced translations from Ronsard and a sonnet "to Sir Ernest Shackleton and his brave companions." Sir Ernest was a particular hero of the girls of Godolphin, as he had lectured there before starting on his voyage in 1907 which would lead to locating the South Magnetic Pole. This would have been before Dorothy went to the school, so she must have caught her enthusiasm from others. The sonnet is stirringly patriotic but not particularly inspiring.

Toward the end of 1910 Miss Douglas made one of her rare errors by appointing Dorothy as house prefect. For a comparative newcomer to be exalted above girls who had been at the school for years caused resentment and made her more unpopular than she was already. She had, for most of her life, little feeling for young children, little understanding of those less intellectually gifted than herself. In later life she knew well how children ought to be taught and dealt with in theory, but always found the actual child before her somewhat daunting. As a prefect she was bossy, with a cutting sarcastic wit. She considered herself the intellectual equal of the mistresses and only they, in her opinion, were worth talking to. "Sucking up" was the verdict of the underlings. She took piano lessons with Fraülein Fehmer, with whom, of course, she was able to converse freely in German. She must have been a sheet anchor to that lonely foreign lady marooned among the English barbarians. Dorothy never lost touch with her, and continued to write to her as long as it was possible to do so, in the hate-ridden days of the First World War. Afterwards, in the terrible starvation that followed because of the Allied blockade of Germany, she sent her food parcels via friends in France, and never failed to give Fraülein Fehmer copies of her books as they were published.

In the spring term of 1911 a vicious form of measles swept through the school. Dorothy, whose childhood had been remarkably healthy, was one of the victims. The disease left her looking like something thrown up by a famine, and almost completely bald. For such a thing to happen to any eighteen-year-old girl would be traumatic. To one already sensitive about her height, her glasses and general clumsiness, it was devastating. For the rest of her life, whenever she was unduly worried or ill, her hair would again give her trouble. This was no doubt an inherited tendency, as her mother suffered in much the same way. She met this crisis, as she was to meet others, with courage and defiance. She bought a wig and returned to classes, played the violin in the orchestra and sang alto in the choir. But it was all too much of a strain. She had put up with Godolphin for two years, hating it and her contemporaries, because the only alternative was Bluntisham, which she disliked almost as much, and because her education was costing her father money. Before the end of the term she suffered a complete breakdown and was removed to a nursing home in Salisbury.

She did not return to Godolphin, and the school, despite her dislike for it, was loath to lose her:

We thought she was going to bring honour to her school and win a scholarship to Oxford. She had great gifts, quite unusual gifts and she made good use of them. . . . None of her work is lost. She has been magazine editor, and has thrown herself into the interests of the school.

Dorothy had known that the best way to get through a time you do not like is to make it go quickly by being as busy as possible.

She returned home, and from there worked for her Oxford scholarship. The next year she went up to Somerville as a Gilchrist scholar.

3

Oxford
and Especially Somerville

The moonlight over Radcliffe Square,
  Small sunset spires that drowse and dream
Thin bells that ring to evening prayer,
  Red willow roots along the stream,
And perilous grey streets, that teem
  With light feet wandering unaware,
And winter nights with lamps agleam,
  Globed golden in the violet air;

Odd nightmare carven things, that stare
  Spell-stricken in a voiceless scream,
The worn steps of an ancient stair,
  With oaken balustrade and beam—
Such things are weightier than they seem,
  These marks my branded soul must bear,
Pledges that Time cannot redeem.
  And yet God knows if I shall care!

Dorothy L. Sayers, "Lay IX." *Op I*

Somerville College was founded in 1879, and by 1912 its third
principal, Miss Emily Penrose, had been in charge for five years.
In the early days there were no resident tutors and the ladies

were escorted to lectures in the men's colleges by respectable chaperones who did their knitting and needlework while their charges imbibed higher education. By 1912, however, Somerville was run in the same way as the rest of the University, with its own staff and all the rest. The curriculum and examinations differed in no way from those which men took, but Oxford was to hold out until 1920 before it gave women degrees. One vestige of Victorian days still remained: no lady could entertain a gentleman in her room, not even a brother or father, without the presence of another lady as chaperone. The term that Dorothy arrived saw the opening of new buildings and the enlargement of the college.

Thirty-three years is not long for an institution to establish itself in an ancient university town. In many ways Somerville was still feeling its way and trying to justify its existence. Higher education for women was not completely accepted in the country at large, and, of course, women still had no vote. Those working hardest for the rights of women were from the universities, and they claimed, among other things, that women, if given power, could be as responsible as were men. It was a touchy time, and Somerville wondered during the next three years if their student Dorothy Leigh Sayers was "good for their image."

She was loud and boisterous, and gathered around her a rebellious clique. In her first year she was still suffering from baldness and wore an untidy straight-cut wig, topped by a great black bow. Moreover, she had been seen loping down the High Street smoking a cigar! She gave out that she was an agnostic and attended chapel only after loud protests. She was never, from infancy even, a non-believer, but no doubt the services in the college chapel were dreary, and how shocking it was for a clergyman's daughter to question the faith! She cut lectures and *talked* in the Bodleian. Much would have been forgiven her if she had been obviously brilliant, but in her first year she did not appear to be so. To get through initial exams she had to attend a crammer in Greek, and, most surprisingly, Latin, in spite of her father's early teaching. Nor did her tutors think much of her English. "She should resist the temptation to be 'smart,' " commented Miss Bruce. "She is bright and clever and has a good deal of personality," conceded Miss Benthorn, but she added, "she is somewhat lacking in self restraint." Miss Jourdain (who saw ghosts at Versailles) pinpointed the faults Dorothy was never quite able to overcome: "At worst she runs off with rhetoric or journalistic slang, or a pulpit manner and spoils her style."

It could be said that if you were a clergyman's daughter a "pulpit manner" was likely to be hereditary. It is true the Reverend Henry Sayers marched about in his study while composing his sermons, but his style of delivery was anything but declamatory. Her mother was a quiet, slyly humorous person, so it is odd that their offspring should have gained such a reputation for boisterousness. In many ways she was still immature. Apart from her father and cousin, and the gardener's boy, who did not count, she had little contact with the opposite sex. Clergymen, as with the Brontë family, did not count either. Many girls, normal girls not in the least inclined to lesbianism, go through a period of hating themselves for being women, and adopt boyish habits to gain attention. This usually occurs around thirteen to sixteen years, and the wise parent will just ride out the storm. With Dorothy it occurred in her late teens. By her second year she was less outrageous, but still given to the weirdest garments and adornments; she would *not* be ignored. She appeared at breakfast in what appeared to be a purple cassock, fished out no doubt from the rectory cupboards, a pair of ornaments consisting of highly-colored parrots in gold wire cages worn as earrings, and a scarlet three-inch-wide ribbon around her head. Miss Penrose was seen to pale, but wisely refrained from giving Dorothy any satisfaction by making public comment. Instead she merely suggested to a third-year student that

Miss Sayers might tactfully be persuaded that her costume was unsuitable for an early-morning lecture.

Now Dorothy was writing poetry and joining in debates. The somewhat unworldly Miss Bruce recorded, "Miss Sayers took a lively part in the discussion, was always to the point and often suggestive." (!) Miss Bruce goes on rather strangely, "She has a good critical power, but strikes me as being somewhat wanting in imagination."

To us who now know the wide range of Dorothy's work, this remark sounds ridiculous, but Miss Bruce had only her college work to judge her by and in a sense she was right. Dorothy was to become a writer on a variety of subjects, but they were subjects of which she had personal knowledge, or had studied in detail. She created little from within her own mind. In 1913 she was still behaving like an overgrown schoolgirl.

It was world events, as well as her own common sense, which eventually almost tamed her. Like the cat, an animal she dearly loved, she tolerated, rather than embraced, civilization. At the end of the summer term of 1914 a grand dance was held at Somerville to celebrate the finishing of the new buildings. Dorothy played the violin in the orchestra. She preferred this to dancing, as her height made it difficult to find partners. Before another year was out most of the young men who had caught her eye as they waltzed and fox-trotted Miss Penrose's young ladies around the hall were dead.

Dorothy had been in France when war broke out and had reached home only after difficulty. The trains had been commandeered to move troops, the cross-Channel boats were crowded with returning English. She went back to a strange Oxford, not yet as empty of men as it was to become, but the thoughts of everyone seemed to be over the Channel. She concentrated on her French and German. "Her *Chanson de Roland* shows some promise of distinction," declared Miss Pope.

Dorothy does not appear to have shown any desire to drop

everything to nurse the wounded in France, as did Vera Brittain and Winifred Holtby later on. In any case, her eyesight would have failed the test. What she did do was to fall desperately in love. She had naturally, with her background of church music and fine alto voice, joined the Bach choir. The conductor then was Dr. (later Sir) Hugh Allen, and Dorothy adored him. Whether or not he was aware of his worshiper no one knows, but the rest of the choir were, and found the sight of this ungainly girl, gazing with wonder at her adored one, extremely comical. She was now a senior student, and as such should have commanded a certain amount of respect, and it may be that the realization that she was not getting this made her take herself in hand. In her efforts to get over her "pash" on Dr. Allen she became extremely bossy and, as a fellow student says, "power mad." Her opportunities, however, for wielding power were slight. She was, it was true, the Bicycle Secretary, probably because no one else would take on this onerous chore. Bicycles were, and probably still are, both a blessing and a bane to colleges. Students will leave them about, to the hazard of townsfolk and aging dons, then complain wildly that they have been stolen. Previous Bicycle Secretaries at Somerville had yelled themselves hoarse trying to get the owners of the machines to park them in the places provided, not on the tennis courts, in the kitchen doorway, or in the corridors. In her term of office Dorothy changed all that; she impounded the errant bicycles and released them only on payment of a fine to the Red Cross. Her title was changed from Bicycle Secretary to Bicycle Tyrant, and the freeways of Somerville were really free.

In March 1915 the War Office inspected Somerville and promptly commandeered it for use as a military hospital. An opening was made to the Radcliffe Infirmary next door through which patients were wheeled to and from the operating theater. For the last party before the soldiers took over Dorothy and others arranged a kind of detective game of hide-and-seek. One of the clues was the finding of an unknown body in a bath. Whether or not the original idea was Dorothy's own she certainly took it over, and the mystery of the body in the bath was the subject of her first full-length Peter Wimsey story. Somerville rented the St. Mary Hall Quadrangle from Oriel College for the rest of the war. St. Mary's, known as Skimmery's, had little room for the accommodation of students, so that for her final term Dorothy was obliged to live in lodgings. All this could have been most unsettling, but Dorothy did not allow it to interfere with her final exams, in which she gained a first class honors degree in French. The examiners went out of their way to publish a rare tribute to her French prose composition, saying that, in their opinion, it had been unsurpassed in distinction of elegance, gaiety, and style.

It was the custom at Somerville, until it died a natural death in 1933, for the third-year students to put on a "Going Down Play." Very trivial affairs for the most part, but great fun for the participants. That of 1915 proves one thing, that Dorothy had controlled her yearning for Dr. Hugh Allen and was able to laugh at herself. The play was in various hands, as was the custom, and was called *Pied Pipings or the Innocents Abroad.* It would come under the heading of "trivia" but that its theme is strangely modern.

The students about to take schools [exams] are in despair because their tutors and examiners are constantly making new discoveries and discrediting traditional views of the subjects they have studied. The Piper, a fairy godfather of Petipa the heroine, leads them to the Never Land where the researchers and experts are confronted with "defunct celebrities"—Alfred the Great, Shakespeare etc.—who confound their critics. The latter do not enjoy themselves and ask to be taken back to Oxford, but the Piper says this is impossible. They themselves have now become defunct and younger scholars are already engaged in controversy about *them*—were they real or mythical people? Did they part their hair in the middle or at the side etc. Petipa pleads with the

Piper to let them return if they promise never to research into things no one wants to know.

Like most undergraduate romps the play is bright and clever, full of "in" jokes and not particularly original. The songs are written to popular tunes, mostly from Gilbert and Sullivan. Dorothy was the musical director and played the leading part, the Pied Piper, Dr. H. P. Rallentando, shamelessly modeled on and made up to resemble Dr. Hugh Allen. Thus she laughed out her passion, and in a song based on "I've Got a Little List" from the *Mikado* she listed her faults for others' amusement. It is called "The Bicycle Secretary's Song." After castigating the bicycle culprits she goes on:

> But these are not the only pests who poison College life,
> And I've made a little list.
> Of those who shake the midnight air with dialectic strife,
> And who never would be missed.
> The nymphs who stroll at breakfast time in nightgowns
>   made of silk;
> The blighters who drop catalogues and whisper in the Bod,
> Or whistle Bach or Verdi as they walk across the Quad,
> The superficial sceptic or the keen philanthropist
> They'll none of them be missed.

It may be a saving grace to publicly, and humorously, acknowledge one's faults, but it can also discomfit other people. There must have been a few red faces in the audience when they realized that their complaints and gossiping had actually reached the target.

It is difficult to know from her later writings if she really liked the University or her college. Apart from *Gaudy Night,* which will be dealt with later, she has not all that much to say about Somerville. She was a guest speaker at the Gaudy of 1934 in which she spoke of Oxford as "the natural home of those who love learning for its own sake, as the forger of minds which are useful in such places as an advertising office." She was chairman of the Somerville College Association of Senior Members 1935–37 but the place does not seem to have entered her soul, and her relationship with her college was always a bit off-hand. Somerville certainly never cared a great deal for her, particularly after *Gaudy Night.* She wrote a "going down" poem which seems to sum up her feelings at this time:

> Now that we have all gone down—have all gone down,
> I will not hold too closely to the past,
> Till it become my staff, or even at last
> My crutch, and I be made a helpless clown.

> All men must walk alone, not drowse, nor drown
> Their wits, with spells of dead things overcast,
> Now that we have gone down, have all gone down,
> I would not hold too closely to the past.

> Therefore, God love thee, thou enchanted town,
> God love thee, leave me, clutch me not so fast;
> Lest, clinging blindly we but grope aghast,
> Sweet friends, go hence and seek your own renown,
> Now that we have gone down—have all gone down.

It is a little sad, but more for Oxford itself than for Somerville. Dorothy Sayers was leaving in triumph, her first class degree had confounded those who doubted her ability in her first year and those who thought she was too flamboyant to be a really good scholar. She did not know what she wanted to do except to please herself, and that was the last thing open to her. She had to earn a living or get married. Her passion for Dr. Hugh Allen had prevented her considering any young man as a prospective husband. The one or two she had liked in her first year were in France or dead. Traveling was out of the question until the war ended, so there was nothing for it but to go back to Bluntisham and hope something would turn up.

4

Early Love and First Works

I only ask that what we shall see shall correspond to
  something,
Beautiful or terrible, but constant in some way or other.
We build the house of thought, stone upon stone,
And just as we have finished the topmost pinnacle
There comes a grinning doubt and pulls away the foundation.
One has to assume something before one can think at all.

Dorothy L. Sayers, *He That Should Come*

After Oxford, Bluntisham must have seemed tamer than ever.
Dorothy dutifully helped her mother with Red Cross fêtes,
joined the sewing and knitting parties, but they were only ways
of passing time. Many afternoons were spent idly lying on her
bed, reading Arthur Conan Doyle and Edgar Wallace, or just
dreaming, dreaming. She always felt guilty when she met her
weary, hard-working father at dinner. Neither parent ever
chided her for her idleness, and because of their patient understanding she felt even more out of love with herself. She wrote

24

poetry, passionately religious verse at odds with her outward pose. As was expected of the rector's daughter, she went to church, and at this time was a great asset to the choir. She did not, however, give the appearance of being particularly devout. There are echoes of Donne in some of the poems written at this time.

> Go, bitter Christ, grim Christ! haul if Thou wilt
> Thy bloody Cross to Thine own bleak Calvary!
> When did I bid Thee suffer for my guilt
> To bind intolerable claims on me?
> I loathe Thy sacrifice; I am sick of Thee.

She had managed to conquer her unsuitable, unrewarded passion for Dr. Hugh Allen, to make a public laughingstock of it at Somerville, and now turned her passion to a love of Christ. But it was a barren time. It was as if she were saying, "I *must* love Christ, for there is no one else."

Later on she was to renew her friendships with some of her Oxford contemporaries, and to keep a few of them as friends until she died, but in spite of her masculine style of dress, which became more pronounced as she grew older, there is no evidence that she was ever *in love* with a woman. Indeed, had she noticed such tendencies in herself she would have fought against them, for any kind of homosexuality was the "unmentionable" sin in the circle in which she had been raised. However broad-minded she was to become later in life, as a young girl the only permissible love was that between members of opposite sexes. At that time she could have been innocent of all sexual knowledge, but by the time she wrote *Unnatural Death* she knew all about lesbianism.

Mary Whittaker is quite the nastiest of her villains and is obviously a lesbian, as clever old Miss Climpson noticed. "I must say, I think it rather *unhealthy*," she writes to Wimsey about the friendship between Miss Whittaker and one of her victims, Vera Findlater. "You may remember Miss Clemence Dane's *very clever book* on the subject?—I have seen so *much* of that kind of thing in my rather WOMAN-RIDDEN existence!" And again, when she tries to advise Vera, "Love is always good, when it's the *right kind*. . . . I cannot help feeling that it is more natural—more proper, in a sense—for a man and woman to be all in all to one another than for two persons of the same sex. Er—after all, it is a—a *fruitful* affection . . . and—and all that."

If Miss Climpson is not explicit enough, then nothing could be plainer than an episode in chapter XV when Wimsey, disguised as Mr. Templeton, and Mary Whittaker, disguised as Mrs. Forrest, meet in the latter's flat. The reason she has engineered this meeting is not absolutely clear; presumably she was intending to "do him in." She makes flagrant advances to him, much puzzling the noble sleuth, but he decides to play her along.

He pulled her suddenly and violently to him, and kissed her mouth with a practised exaggeration of passion.

He knew then. No one who has ever encountered it can ever again mistake that awful shrinking, that uncontrollable revulsion of the flesh against a caress that is nauseous. He thought for a moment that she was going to be actually sick.

In 1915 Wimsey was still in the future. What Dorothy had to do now was to find a job, and for an honors graduate there was little else but teaching. She was not overjoyed at the prospect, but dutifully sent her name and qualifications to the scholastic agencies. She was offered the post of modern language teacher at Hull High School for girls, one within the control of the Church Schools Company Ltd. To many people Hull is acceptable only if you call it Kingston-upon-Hull. They imagine it as nothing but a windswept fish market where the only utterance is "Ee ba goom." If Dorothy thought of it like that she was in for a pleasant surprise. Her rooms at 80 Westbourne Avenue looked out on to a quiet tree-lined road. If the wind was in the wrong direction the whole town was permeated with the smell of fish, but who could resent that when it was fish that had built it and made it the largest port of its kind in the world? People could *pay* for things in Hull, including their daughters' educations. Dorothy would have admired its vast Holy Trinity Church, and St. Mary's with the footpath running through the tower, and been fascinated by its old streets such as The Land of Green Ginger, which sounds like the title of a children's fairy tale, and indeed, was to be used later as a book title by Winifred Holtby. She would have visited Wilberforce's birthplace, and admired Hull's sturdy independence. Even now it has its own private telephone company.

Until fairly recently anyone with a degree, even someone who had failed to get into any other profession, could get a job as a teacher without ever having been *taught* to teach. Many of our better known writers started that way, and some, like Evelyn Waugh, made marvelous copy from their experiences. Unless the graduate was also a natural, a born teacher, however, the experience could have been hell. In later years Dorothy seldom mentioned her time at Hull, which could mean that it was so terrible she wanted to forget it, or that it made little impression upon her. Since she "wrote out" in some way all the unpleasantnesses of her life she probably enjoyed the years 1915–17 as best she could. Certainly she made her mark as a teacher, for she is still vividly remembered by quite a few of her ex-pupils. "She was so different from the usual staff—so gay and attractive—she dressed well and moved quickly," writes one of them nearly sixty years later. Her hair had now grown long enough to be worn in the current "ear phones" style. Her bubbling laughter was infectious, and the understanding smile, with those deep dimples, gave confidence to many an awkward, uncertain teen-age girl.

"Of *course* you can write a Latin verse," she would declare, and they found they could, after a fashion. They could also compose playlets in French, which they had never tried before. No one laughed louder at their mistakes than the mistress, so that all their lives they would remember the difference between a pig and a coachman, whatever else they forgot. They even became proficient enough to stage Molière's *Les Précieuses ridicules* in public, to aid the Red Cross. She had no favorites, so that even the most shy, unspectacular child felt at ease with her. Not long after she joined the school she began to behave in the school assembly in what the girls thought a very strange way. Instead of taking her place at the end of the row of her girls, she took a different position each day. What she was seeking were voices for the choir she intended forming, and it was typical of her methods that she should use this way instead of announcing voice trials. Her choice was announced: "You and you and you can *sing*, I've heard you in assembly." Much less time was wasted than listening to those who wanted to shine but were tone deaf and trying to bludgeon others to open their mouths. She just had to bully the ones she knew could form the nucleus of a choir. This choir flourished during her time at the school and added greatly to the quality of assembly.

But Dorothy was not content as a schoolmistress. Although her unorthodox methods were enjoyed by the girls, they were not always approved by her fellow teachers. She was opinionated and argumentative, probably better educated than most of her colleagues, and would let them know it. Although she got on very well with the girls, she did not care for "unformed" minds. Small children actually terrified her, and she continued to find it very difficult to bend her mind to the less intellectually able.

The year 1917 was one of change for the Sayers family. Her father came to an agreement with the rector of Christchurch, near Wisbech, to exchange livings. The rector there, Mr. Neville, had a bigger family and needed a bigger income. So the Reverend Henry—one of God's fools if ever one existed—took a £200-a-year cut in his stipend and moved a few miles further east, deeper into the Fens. Dorothy described Christchurch as "the last place God made, and when He finished it He found He'd forgotten the staircase." It was even worse than Bluntisham, which at least was on a fairly well used road; Christchurch was an enclave within an enclave. It had the old Vermuyden Drain to the south, the Hundred Foot Drain to the east and the Sixteen Foot Drain to the west. It is now possible to get to the village from three different directions, but in 1917 there was only one fairish road, winding out from Downham Market, and a couple of tracks, often impassable in winter. It is difficult to see how a community of eight hundred souls was ever established there at all, but it was considered important enough in 1861 for a church to be built there. Giles Scott, who built St. Pancras Station and Hotel, is credited with the design of it, which probably means that it came from a stock design in his office and he may have had no hand in it himself. It is a mean little red brick building with an even meaner red brick rectory. To Dorothy, who loved soaring vaults and angel roofs, whose first experience of church had been in the glorious Christchurch Cathedral in Oxford, to come to red brick and pitch pine pews must have been a terrible letdown. But there was no arguing with that stubborn, saintly father of hers. Even with a £200 drop the living was good, though never enough to satisfy the Reverend Henry's charitable urges. There was still space enough in the rectory for his study, her aunt's sitting room and her mother's den, and for Dorothy's bed-sitting room, looking towards the wood. She filled the shelves with her copies of the works of Arthur Conan Doyle, Edgar Wallace, and every other book about crime and crime writing she could find, as well as the classics and a little pile of her own slim volume of verse, *Op I,* which Blackwell's had published in 1916. This room was to see the birth of *Whose Body?* and *Clouds of Witness,* both written under stress in 1921 and 1923 respectively.

Many years later she was to set what I feel was not only her best detective story, but probably the best *ever* detective story, *The Nine Tailors,* in and around Christchurch, but just now the place had no charms for her. She did little but lie around or stride alone about the countryside during her holidays, scandalizing her father's parishioners by being seen sitting on a gate and *smoking.* It is odd now to remember how much people were shocked, a comparatively short time ago, by the sight of a lady walking alone in the country and by women who smoked.

The days were not entirely lost. She had been able to hand in her notice at Hull, for Basil Blackwell had offered to teach her the publishing trade; she was to earn her keep as his reader. All she was waiting for was to hear about digs, then she would be off again to Oxford, the city of golden youth, ever-chiming bells and the Bach choir. There were some interesting people she had met in her final year who would still be at Somerville, like Margaret Kennedy and Helen Pybus.

Meanwhile she was preparing another book of poems for Blackwell's. This firm of publishers and booksellers brought out a number of slim volumes of verse during the war years, quite a few of them by women undergraduates. They were made in hand-printed style by the Vincent Press and bound in brown paper, or stiff card covers. *Op I* had been ninth in the series *Adventurers All*—"a series of young poets unknown to fame." Volume seven was *The Burning Wheel* by A. L. Huxley; T. W. Earp contributed volume four, but the rest remained "unknown to fame," as poets at any rate. The object of the series was "to remove from the work of young poets the reproach of insolvency. The series will be confined to such work as would seem to deserve publicity. It is hoped that these Adventurers may justly claim the attention of those intellects which, in resisting the enervating influence of the novel, look for something of permanent value in the more arduous pursuit of poetry."

Such high-flown hopes were vain, for almost every "adventurer" who made the literary grade made it as a novelist and not as a poet; but for all that, someone should one day write the "Basil Blackwell Story" and give him his rightful place in the literary scene. Dorothy's second book of verse for him was called *Catholic Tales and Christian Songs* and came out in 1918. It was an odd and misleading title. The word *Catholic*, more so fifty years ago than now, meant, to the majority of people, Roman Catholic. In spite of a report in the *New York Times* when she died, she never joined, or, so far as I can discover, contemplated joining the Roman Catholic Church. The cover bears a woodcut of Christ crucified and crowned in glory, which must also have misled readers. The poems are, however, all about Christ, but some of them, notably the one quoted earlier, must have shocked many Christians, Anglican or Roman, especially coming, as one critic said, "from the pen of a lady." Several hark back to Donne, others suggest the influence of *Idylls of the King* and Hilaire Belloc, from whom the title is derived.

In *The Mind of the Maker*, published in 1941, she refers to "a youthful set of stanzas" ("The Carpenter's Son") from this book, and says, "I should not write it quite like that today. . . . But the end is clearly there in the beginning. It would not be quite exact to say that the wheel has come full circle." At that time she was involved with religious drama and had completely given up detective writing. She was quite right, the end was in the beginning, for *Catholic Tales* contains a playlet which leaps forward over twenty years to *The Man Born to Be King*. It is called *The Mocking of Christ* and it shows the figure of Jesus set up by soldiers to play a game called "Jesus Christ is Lord of All." The Pope, the King, the Preacher, the Patriot and others dress the figure in turn according to their own tastes. He gets crowned, slapped on the back by a hearty curate, given tea by a meek one, and wound in red tape by a respectable gentleman. Artistically and dramatically it goes on too long; as her Oxford tutors complained, Dorothy never knew what to leave out. But it would make a telling and amusing sketch today. In 1918 it shocked people even to read it, and no one would have allowed it to be performed, however reverentially, in a church. She wrote no overt war poems, and indeed nothing whatever about the war while she was living through it. This may be what Miss Bruce meant when she said "she doesn't seem to have much imagination." Her imagination was there all right, but it preferred to dwell in the past, with knights and quests and classical sagas; it could not encompass the fearful present. Besides, people at home were kept in ignorance of the real horrors of the front, and the great poets were either dead or not yet published. In fact the real enormity of the horror of that war is still unfolding, nearly sixty years later. Dorothy had not the kind of imagination that reached out beyond what she was doing from day to day; but she did have the kind which could blot out what she did not want to know. The Oxford to which she returned in 1917 was a grayer place than the city she had left two years earlier. Somerville was still in exile at Skimmery's, and most of the students in lodgings. There were hardly any young men. Where the golden boys had congregated in noisy gaggles were knots of crippled, pale men in hospital blue.

She joined the Bach choir again and went around with them, singing to the troops and to the aged in the Infirmary. She was surprised to find how maudlin, in the matter of hymns, were the old and simple people. "Their first choice was 'A few more years shall roll' and the second was like unto it, namely, 'Within the churchyard side by side.' Since then I have been chary of considering what people may reasonably be expected to like, and have contented myself with observing what they do, in fact, like; after which I please myself about giving or withholding it."

She threw herself into her work at Blackwell's, chattering and arguing incessantly. She became friends with Doreen Wallace, then in her second year at Somerville, who had digs near her own in Bath Place. Doreen was a good match for Dorothy. Also tall and slim, with a rapier-like mind, she had an easy command of language. Her father claimed descent from Wallace the Scottish patriot, and some of her childhood had been spent with dour Scots aunts. Doreen could both encourage Dorothy in her nonsense, for her own amusement, and deflate her with one short wicked sentence. They would argue for hours, Dorothy the Christian, back in the fold after her flirtation with agnosticism, and Doreen the unbeliever, neither moving one inch from her stance. They were both fairly penniless, Dorothy more so than Doreen, as her pay from Blackwell's was microscopic; she was, after all, supposed to be learning a trade. An allowance was sent to her from home, but this covered only the necessities of board and lodging. Most of her dresses were black. Gone were the days of the purple cassock; it had to be black in the stern working world, and besides, black hid the dirt. But it was *dull*. Doreen hit on the idea of cutting out a large Tudor rose from some stout red cotton material, and stitching it on to the front of one of these dresses. A smaller version was then fixed to her black floppy felt hat. This enlivened the scene a little, but not half so much as Dorothy's rendering of "Fling wide the gates, the Saviour waits!" while striding down the High. When she wanted to illustrate a point she never bothered to consider her surroundings. People would turn and stare, but eccentrics were commonplace on the Oxford scene. So she jogged on, polishing her book of poems, trying to make sense of the publisher's office, until 1918, when again she was smitten by a grand passion.

Eric Whelpton had returned to Oxford after being invalided from the army. The war had left him a prey to nerves and nightmares but not wounded. The four years had taught him that he was extremely attractive to women. For one who was, as he says, "cursed by a middle-class upbringing," he found the wartime women almost as shocking as the war itself. With the end of the world for so many at hand, the desire of women to "give their all" to the men they loved seemed to sweep through the middle and upper classes. For many others it was not a matter of sacrificing virtue but of losing it to any man who would take it for the sake of some kind of experience before the human race was completely destroyed. A "fine upstanding man" still alive at twenty-four could live the life of the idealized romantic sheik if he so desired, and for free.

Doreen Wallace, Dorothy L. Sayers and Eric Whelpton all had rooms in or near Bath Place. Doreen met and chatted to anyone on any pretext and in this way had met Eric going to and from lectures. She introduced the tall, dark, pale-faced, Byronic-type hero to Dorothy, and from then on Miss Sayers was lost. He could not walk down the street without being panther-tracked by his adorer, who could watch his comings and goings from her sitting-room window. Should he go to the Bodleian, sure enough the black hat would bob up from one of the booths. Dorothy threw herself at him and got very little in exchange, even on the intellectual level. Whelpton was a fine linguist, and had an easy prose style, but he had little interest in the higher flights of learning, and none in religion. A contemporary remembers him as a "big beautiful sexpot," and Dorothy was not the only one to fall for him. However, she was the most blatant and persistent, even carrying him out of Doreen's orbit, a fact which might have ruined their friendship. This was to last though for a few years yet, and Doreen, who had little trouble finding male admirers, let this one go with an amused shrug.

There is nothing more ridiculous than a plain, intense woman throwing herself at an uninterested man. She is the subject of hundreds of comedies, and audiences have rolled in the aisles at her situation; but is there anything more tragic, more likely to leave a scar on the soul? Whatever Whelpton did, Dorothy

Eric Whelpton, 1917

would be hurt. He was too much of a "gentleman" to ignore her entirely; besides, when she was not being demanding and tearful, she was great fun to be with. But every kindness on his part, every shared pot of tea in the Cadena Café, every embrace it was impossible to evade without giving insult only increased her longing. Her work at Blackwell's suffered, and it was becoming obvious that she was not cut out for a publisher's office. Suddenly her realism came to her rescue. Eric, who hated scenes, summoned enough courage to tell her that the case was hopeless. He was in love, he said "wildly, passionately, irretrievably" with someone else. It all sounds like an offering from the Romantic Novelists' Association.

Dorothy's love did not run away to nothing, of course. It was to pay handsome dividends later on, but for now she recognized defeat, came to an amicable arrangement with Blackwell's, and left Oxford in the early days of peace.

Now she went abroad for a bit, and then home to Christchurch. Knowing how desperately in love with him she had been, Whelpton's next move sounds nothing short of cruel. He had been offered a post at Les Roches in southern France, a snobbish French boys' school equivalent to Eton, and he needed an administrative assistant. There was Dorothy, out of work, fluent in the language, who would do anything for him, and who, moreover, was no rival to the woman with whom he was infatuated. Eric offered her the job, and was somewhat surprised when she did not leap at it straight away. He would have to spend a weekend at Christchurch, to be inspected by the family. Writing from her old digs in Hull where she had gone for a visit, she addressed him as "Dear Mr. Whelpton," as if they had scarcely ever met. Her parents must have approved of the scheme, for on August 18, 1919, Eric and Dorothy set off together for France. They cycled most of the way and put up at lodgings approved by the Cyclists' Touring Club.

At Les Roches Dorothy was in charge of a house set apart

from the main building, and for all she saw of Eric he might have been in Timbuktu. The whole thing fell to pieces within a year. Eric's fatal charm had captivated the exceedingly ugly daughter of the proprietor, and in the Gallic manner her father had offered Eric a partnership free, if he would marry the girl. Looking upon this as a "fate worse than death," Eric fled back to England, leaving Dorothy to pick up the pieces and his luggage and follow in an orderly manner at the term's end. Eric went to Florence to set up as an estate agent and from that time he and Dorothy were to meet on only two occasions.

In 1920 she was again jobless and without a permanent home in London. She joined the first batch of Oxford women ever to be awarded a Master of Arts degree, and had fun renewing old acquaintances and finding that "everybody seems to be engaged or married." And she came to the strange conclusion, after seeing one play at the Little Theatre, that "Englishmen cannot act." "Great excitement caused by *G-H-Q-Love* because the scene is laid in the lavatory," she wrote to Eric, "but after a year's residence at Les Roches I seem to be getting blasé about lavatories. It's a pity to outlive the thrills of one's youth."

Dorothy was now twenty-seven, neither engaged nor married, and not even earning a living. Much of her spare time at Les Roches had been spent reading "Dead-Eye Dick" stories and Arsène Lupin's adventures. When chided, she would say that she was studying the genre, "for that is where the money is." Her colleagues considered this just an excuse for indulging her bad taste. A few jobs as a temporary teacher turned up for her, one of them at the Girls' High School at Clapham, where she amazed the girls by her unorthodox methods. These would have fitted well into the modern idea of teaching, for standing in front of a class and holding forth was not Dorothy's way—she expected the girls to join with her in finding out. In 1920 it left the girls goggle-eyed and the rest of the staff suspicious. One of the pupils remembers: "She grabbed a sword which was on the

mantelpiece of the classroom and stumped up and down between the desks brandishing it above her head, quoting meantime from the *Pirates of Penzance* 'with-cat-like-tread-upon-
our-prey-we-steal.' "

In 1921 Dorothy joined Benson's advertising agency in London. She was engaged as a copywriter at what was a good wage
of around £4 a week—much more than she could get as a
teacher. She was able, with her father's help, to rent a flat in
Great James Street, Bloomsbury, within walking distance of the
office. For longer journeys she invested in a motorcycle, which
she rode with dignity, sitting bolt upright as if driving a chariot.

What the Reverend Henry Sayers thought of his classically
educated daughter as a writer of advertising jingles is not on
record. He may have been disappointed that his investment on
her behalf in Oxford University was paying meager dividends.
He may also have recognized that in spite of her academic
achievements, and in spite of being in sight of thirty, she was
in many respects undeveloped. Then, as she assured everyone,
it was only a stopgap job until she was really established as a
writer. It was a stopgap that was to last ten years.

5

The Business of Advertising and Personal Problems

Of course, there is *some* truth in advertising. There's yeast
in bread. . . . Truth in advertising is like leaven, which a
woman hid in three measures of meal. It provides a suitable
quantity of gas with which to blow out a mass of crude
misrepresentation into a form that the public can swallow.
Dorothy L. Sayers, *Murder Must Advertise*

Benson's was an old established firm whose rather creaking
offices did not match the public's idea of the slick advertising
company. Dorothy's account of it, under the name of Messrs.
Pym, describes the setup exactly as it was. Benson's had, with
great daring, employed their first woman as "ideas man and
copywriter" toward the end of the war, and it was she whom
Dorothy replaced. Dorothy had learned something of lettering
and layout from Blackwell's, and knew a good deal about printers' and publishers' language. She could compose rhymes and
jingles at the drop of a hat, and could make fairly good quick
rough sketches. It was a comfortable, easy-going office, and, if
you fitted in, a very happy one. The characters in *Murder Must
Advertise* are a mixture of her fellow staff. She jumbled up a

trait of this one with the looks of that, but several of them are quite recognizable. The head of her department, Mr. Oswald Greene, came out as Mr. Armstrong, and Mr. Jayne, another copy director, as Mr. Hankin. She wrote herself in as Miss Meteyard, the plain, Oxford-educated copywriter never at a loss for an apt quotation. The great annual event was, as it is in the book, the cricket match, which was played with Virol Limited.

Before she had settled in at Benson's Dorothy had spent some time at home in Christchurch, hammering out a novel in the genre she was quite sure would make the most money—detective fiction. Certainly she was too near disappointed love, and too hurt by it, to try the other sure money maker—the romantic tale. In her striding walks around the village, during the hours she spent sitting on farm gates or lying by the river, forever smoking cigarettes through the long holder she now adopted à la Edgar Wallace, Dorothy had worked on the background of her hero.

She had no personal experience whatsoever of the titled upper classes, but it was their doings, if the newspapers were to be believed, which enthralled everyone. This was before they were superseded by the age of the film stars, who have in turn been supplanted by the pop stars. Dorothy had noticed that most of the nobility who made the headlines were not the dukes and earls themselves, but their younger offshoots. The younger son of a noble house would have the right touch of romance, especially if he were extremely rich in his own right. She called to mind the places round about Christchurch. There was a River Wissey that ran into the Bedford Level; Lord Wissey sounded rather a silly ass, no one would suspect that kind of chap to hide a keen mind and an analytical brain. But it was a little too sibilant; he was to be an unpredictable man, a man of whims and fancies. Whims, Wissey. Take the *h* from one word, and put an *m* in the other—Wimsey. That was it!—son of the late Duke of Denver.

Denver is a village about three miles south of Downham Market, where a distant relative of the Sayers family, Dr. Wells, lived. It was the birthplace of a *real* eccentric, Captain Manby, who invented the breeches buoy and revolutionized safety at sea. The nearest great mansion was Oxburgh Hall and the greater part of Norfolk was still in the hands of titled landowners, so it was a good place to set her hero. Right from the beginning he was intended to be the leading character in a saga, not a one-off affair. When the Duke of Denver is grumbling about his brother's propensity for dabbling in police matters, and getting the family name in the newspapers, Peter retorts, "I'm bein' no end useful. You may come to want me yourself, you never know." Which, of course, the Duke did in the second Wimsey book, *Clouds of Witness.* So it is possible the two stories were going around in Dorothy's head at the same time.

The germ of *Whose Body?* had, as we have seen, its origins at Somerville, from the parlor game in which each participant had to add an incident to a story. Dorothy had provided an unknown body in a bath. *Whose Body?* is a short, highly intelligent book, with a well-constructed story. Wimsey's inner circle is practically complete. Bunter, the manservant; Parker, the Scotland Yard detective; the deceivingly butterfly-minded mother, the Dowager Duchess; and Freddie Arbuthnot, who is "something in the City." Although Wimsey is shown playing Bach and collecting first editions, he is not so heavily loaded with quotations as he was to become. Dorothy placed her hero in Ouida-like surroundings. He had, in fact, a great deal in common with that lady: a Piccadilly flat decorated in primrose and black and furnished with opulent chairs and Chesterfields, the walls lined with first editions and the Sèvres vases filled with bronze chrysanthemums. Wimsey lolled about in purple silk pajamas and a peacock-embroidered dressing gown. Apart from all this chi-chi the book has some strangely careless faults. It is highly unlikely that a butler, even if he did give valuable assistance in the matter of detection, would be paid £200 a year all found in the 1920s. To exhume a corpse and hold a post mortem on it then and there, within sight and hearing of the widow, was scarcely probable, especially as the corpse was in a large number of pieces, having been dissected in the medical school. In this matter several doctors have pointed out that medical students are not given a whole body to divide up between them; they will work altogether on arms or legs, the necessary parts being drawn from the body bank by the attendant to the dissecting room. These errors do not spoil the story or make it impracticable, and the average reader is not familiar with the finer points of law and medicine.

The book begins without any preamble: " 'Oh, damn!' said Lord Peter Wimsey." In those days the word was usually written "D——n". This did not cause nearly so much of a talking point as Michael Arlen's opening of *The Green Hat*—" 'Hell!' said the Duchess"—which came out a year after *Whose Body?* After many stops and starts the book was finished in 1921 and offered to several publishers, who turned it down on the grounds of "coarseness." An American publisher took a chance on it, provided certain matters were cut out. The story concerned the disappearance of a Jewish financier, Sir Reuben Levy. A naked, dead, Semitic-featured gentleman had turned up in a bath and the bumbling Inspector Sugg was anxious to identify him as Levy. Peter Wimsey, however, knew "it to be no go by the evidence of my own eyes." The evidence was, originally, that the body was uncircumcised, which definitely ruled out Sir Reuben Levy, and ruled out the book for acceptance. No doubt she made a fight for her clue, but in the end had to be content with giving the corpse dirty toenails and flea bites, unlikely to be found on a rich, well-cared-for gentleman. Towards the end of the book the medical student, Piggott, says: "Tommy Pringle said the old Sheeny—"

"Why did he call him a Sheeny?" cuts in Wimsey.

"I don't know. But I know he did."

The head, which would have been the only other clue to the corpse's racial identity, had not been worked on by the students.

Dorothy eventually managed to sell the book to Fisher-Unwin. They were taken over by Ernest Benn Limited, who finally brought it out in 1923. It did not shake the earth, but the sales were encouraging enough to carry on with the second Wimsey novel, *Clouds of Witness.*

Somewhat to her surprise, Dorothy was quite enjoying her work at Benson's, though at times feeling a bit guilty about this enjoyment. She was, after all, a scholar, and one part of her longed for the scholar's life, shut away with books from the world. In reality she was much too gregarious for that. She liked being with people, arguing, tossing outrageous advertising jingles around the office. She had fierce debates with Oswald Greene about religion and about the ethics of advertising. It passed the time, but life was also passing by. She was thirty and there seemed no prospect of marriage to relieve her from having to work for her living. Men liked her company, but she did not seem to attract them physically. She was a great "taker-up" of hobbies, throwing herself into them with gusto, talking about them incessantly, bludgeoning others to share her enthusiasm. For a time it was photography; she bought various cameras and gadgets, and spent her lunch hours developing her prints in Benson's dark room. It was not for nothing that Wimsey's man, Bunter, was also an expert photographer. Bunter, however, could persuade his master to buy him every new aid which came on to the market, such as a "Double Anastigmat with a set of supplementary lenses" for £50. When Dorothy had exhausted as much equipment as she could afford she lost interest as a practitioner, but the knowledge she had gained was always to be useful to her detective. She also liked puzzles; when *The Times* first began publishing its crossword puzzles the mania swept through the office, and very little work was done until the day's puzzle was completed.

This was now, of course, the Jazz Age, and Dorothy's violin was not in demand for the firm's dances as it had been at Somerville; but no matter, she acquired a second-hand saxophone, and contributed some spirited "Wa, wa, wa's" to the annual staff romp at Christmas. It was a far cry from Bach or Wimsey's Scarlatti, but it was fun. Bloomsbury and Chelsea teemed with small clubs—literary, Marxist, poetry—wherever two people of like minds met, they formed a club. From the evidence of the Wimsey books Dorothy appears to have known one of these clubs quite well—one founded for Russian sympathizers. The Soviet Club appears in *Clouds of Witness* (1926) and *The Unpleasantness at the Bellona Club* (1928).

The Soviet Club, being founded to accommodate free thinking rather than high living, had that curious amateur air which pervades all worldly institutions planned by unworldly people. Exactly why it made Lord Peter instantly think of mission teas he could not say, unless it was that all the members looked as though they cherished a purpose in life, and that the staff seemed rather sketchily trained and strongly in evidence.

Very nearly all the Sayers books, and many of the short stories, take a swipe at the Red menace, and to the end of her life she firmly believed in "Reds under the bed," but there is another reason they figure in the Wimsey stories. A detective story, which is, in effect, a modern parable of good versus evil, has to have something bad in opposition to the good as personified by the detective. The Reds were the fashionable villains of the twenties, but they do feature sometimes unnecessarily. *Clouds of Witness* would have got along quite well without the side issue of Wimsey's sister's involvement with a Communist; but it does give rise to some very comic dialogue.

"—ever know a sincere emotion to express itself in a subordinate clause?"

"Joyce has freed us from the superstition of syntax," agreed the curly man.

"Scenes which make emotional history," said Miss Heath-Warburton, "should ideally be expressed in a series of animal squeals."

"The D. H. Lawrence formula," said the other.

"Or even Dada," said the authoress.

"We need a new notation," said the curly-haired man. . . .

"Have you ever heard Robert Snoates recite his own verse to the tom-tom and the penny whistle?"

(Clouds of Witness)

All this is Miss Sayers having fun at the expense of the pseudo-intellectuals, and nothing at all to do with the progress of the detective story.

It may have been at one of these clubs that Dorothy met the man who was to change her life, or rather, to prevent her changing it, but to keep her tied to her job and to Wimsey for a further eight years. It is not as yet revealed whether he was a "grand passion," just a casual acquaintance, or someone taken up for the "experience" supposed to be so necessary for the writer. It could have been "Oh to hell with it! I'm past thirty— if I don't find out soon I never will." Whatever the reason for her (to use an old-fashioned word in this context) "yielding," she realized by June 1923 that she was pregnant. In an address called "The Six Other Deadly Sins" given to the Public Morality Council in 1941 she dismisses Lust as the least important of the Seven Deadly Sins.

Men and women may turn to lust in sheer boredom and discontent, trying to find in it some stimulus which is not provided by the drab discomfort of their mental and physical surroundings. When *that* is the case, stern rebukes and restrictions are worse than useless.

However lenient she may have felt toward other people in her middle age, she was profoundly shocked at herself. She confided in no one close to her and, using the as yet unfinished *Clouds of Witness* as an excuse, she asked Benson's for six months' leave from September and went home to Christchurch. In an effort to save every possible penny she eschewed the train and traveled home on her motorcycle, a pretty dangerous procedure for one almost six months advanced in pregnancy. Her parents, expecting her to arrive at about nine o'-clock in the evening, had to sit up until past eleven, worrying and praying for her safety. It is probable that she confided in her parents. They would have had to be extremely unworldly had they not eventually noticed her condition, but by keeping mostly to her own bed-sitting room and adopting a voluminous wrapper from the start, she kept it from everyone else, even the knowing housemaids. At times she sang in the church choir, wearing her M.A. cap and gown. She had made arrangements to have the child in a private nursing home in Bournemouth and went to spend Christmas with a Somerville friend who lived nearby and who must have been the only person with whom Miss Sayers shared her secret. The child was born on January 3, 1924, strangely enough, in the registering district of Christchurch.

One of the enigmas of Dorothy L. Sayers's life is not that she had an illegitimate child but her subsequent treatment of him. She did not like children, professed to abhor babies, and resented the intrusion of this one into her life. That being so, it is strange that she did not take steps to have it adopted. There is no reason, except of course the legal one which is often honored in the breach, why she could not have had it under an assumed name and registered the child in that name. But she registered it on January 28 in her own name, giving her profession as "authoress," and there it is in the public records for anyone with enough curiosity to see. She was familiar enough with the contents of Somerset House, the repository of records of births and deaths, and the ease with which information can be obtained to realize that this was bound to be explored. It is almost as if she purposely left clues. It is sad that both Dorothy and the child might possibly have been happier had she left it on the steps of the Foundling Hospital close by her Bloomsbury flat. What she did do was to put him in the care of an eccentric cousin, and never mention it—ever—not even in conversation with her nearest friends. This, for someone who liked to top all discussions with a "My dear, I *know* . . ." must have called for super-human control. Now she had to have money, not only for herself, but for the upkeep of the child. However, she was to give him little other than what money could buy; nothing whatever of herself. It was as if she had said, "I have had this creature. I should not have done, but having had it, I will see it fed, clothed and educated; but don't ask me to *love* it as well."

With the birth over, the child settled, *Clouds of Witness* finished, she returned to Benson's.

6

The Growth of Wimsey— and Marriage

Has father joined the Mustard Club?
Poster appearing on London buses, 1926

The nineteen-twenties and early thirties saw the heyday of the great advertising campaigns. The most successful seem to have been of the "serial" type of newspaper and magazine advertisement. There was the athletic gentleman who attributed all his prowess to Kruschen Salts. Numerous infants prattled, "Over the fence jumps Sunny Jim, 'Force' is the stuff that raises him," and "Better, oh, better, very much better. Better smoke 'Capstans' they're blended better" along with their nursery rhymes. There was Bateman's man who had "never heard of 'Aspro,'" and there was "George" who had "gone to Lyonch," as well as the Guinness "My goodness!" posters. Many of these campaigns originated with Benson's, but none of them "took off" so successfully as the "Mustard Club." Oddly enough, it came about through a decision of J. & J. Colman's of Norwich to reduce their advertising allocation for mustard, the product through which they were, and still are, most widely known. Their Haslar posters, now collectors' items, were famous, as were their contributions to schools in the way of booklets and wall charts; but none of this did much actually to *sell* mustard. "The difficulty in all our campaigns," admitted Colman's, "is to get our advertisements read. Mustard to the man in the street is, by its nature, a dull subject."

The invention of the Mustard Club is attributed to Oswald Greene himself, though it probably arose out of one of those "ideas" meetings. "It is unreasonable," said Benson's, "that we can interest the man in the street in Mustard for its own sake, or even for the sake of his digestion, for, unlike Americans, the English do not take their digestions seriously." Whoever began it, much of the succeeding copy was written by Dorothy, and her description of the "Whifflets" campaign in *Murder Must Advertise* is very little exaggerated compared with what actually happened to the Mustard Club. What Colman's had envisaged as a holding operation during a time of financial stress became what everyone in advertising dreams about, a self-perpetuating venture. Once the characters were established, adventures about them could run for years; it became so crazy that people were buying newspapers just to read of the doings of the Mustard Club. Its beginning was worthy of any detective story writer. Large posters appeared on the buses and billboards merely saying "Join the Mustard Club," "Mustard Club in Court," "Mustard Club Member Blackballed" and so on. Letters appeared in the press and cartoons in the funny papers, all this before the firm or the actual product was even named.

When, in September 1926, all was revealed, the public was ready to appreciate the joke. Looking at the copy now, the only fascinating things about it are the pen-and-ink drawings by Brealey and J. Gilroy which headed each adventure. These show the authentic dress of the twenties more clearly than do contemporary photographs. Some of the humor was a bit overweighted with puns: the president of the Club was the Baron de Beef, of Porterhouse College, Cambridge, and the secretary, Miss Di Gester. What sounds like a typical Dorothy L. Sayers effort appeared under the heading "Mustard and Matrimony" and began:

> At Baconwell Police Court a case was brought by Mrs. E. N. Pecker, of Nag's Head Lane, Barking, who complained of cruelty on the part of her husband. He was liverish, she said, and used words to her and was round at his club every evening.
> The Magistrate: Was it the Mustard Club? (laughter).
> Complainant: No, he always came back in such a bad temper that she thought it must be a political club.

Of course the couple are reconciled in the end through the intervention of Lady Hearty, an officer of the Mustard Club. The thing about these advertisements is that they contradict the canon of advertising law, that the product being advertised must immediately hit the reader in the eye. These things had to be actually *read,* and Dorothy always had a theory that you could get anyone to read anything if it was made interesting enough—a theory she was to put into practice in particular when she came to translating Dante, but which is also borne out in the Wimsey books.

Famous British stage stars such as Delysia, Leslie Henson and Phyllis Titmus lent their names to the advertisements, as did the restaurants Simpsons and the Café Royal. The great joke of the day was, "What is a canary? Answer. A sparrow who has joined the Mustard Club." Up and down the country small children were entered in fancy dress competitions as mustard pots, and in Elgin six tots appeared as the Mustard Club committee (along with Felix the Cat and the Ku-Klux-Klan!).

It was all good fun while it lasted—about two years—and helped to brighten up the country then in the dual grip of strikes and national unrest. These were the years, during which Dorothy was probably at her happiest, which saw the publication of *Clouds of Witness, Unnatural Death, The Unpleasant-*

ness at the Bellona Club and a volume of short stories. Her reputation as a detective story writer was firmly established, and on April 13, 1926, she had married. Whatever happened now, she would never follow the path of those spinster aunts and cousins; she had a man of her own.

As the years went by her friends were to wonder, why this particular man? Oswald Arthur Fleming was born in Kirkwall on November 6, 1881. He was to pose as an Orcadian of ancient lineage, but actually his being born in the Orkneys was an accident of his father's occupation. John Fleming was a customs officer and it was unusual for anyone in this service to stay in one place for very long. He had married Jane Peebles Maconochie in Edinburgh three months before the boy was born, so that Oswald was only technically legitimate. This fact, together with the wandering life of a customs officer's family, may have had an unsettling effect on the boy, but could not, in itself, have been responsible for his penchant for self-dramatizing fantasy. When he was seventeen he altered his very ordinary name to Oswold (with two *o*'s) and the undistinguished Arthur to Atherton. With these embellishments he joined the 4th Durham Light Infantry, but was discharged a year later "in order to proceed to South Africa." As he did not go to South Africa, where there was a war raging, in any military capacity, it may have been another move to follow the flag of the customs office. It was in Africa that he worked in a newspaper office for a short time, a stint for which he glorified himself later as "a war correspondent." His warrior's tales depicted himself as a dashing major in the Royal Dragoons, the original of Beau Geste in the French Foreign Legion, the slaughterer of countless "Jerries," and the victim of shell shock. His official army record is a little more prosaic. He served in the Royal Army Service Corps from May 17, 1915 to January 7, 1919. He relinquished his commission "on the grounds of ill-health contracted on army service," and retained the rank of captain. His ill health does not appear to have merited a pension, and his only awards were the 1914–15 star, the British war medal, and the victory medal, which were given to every serving soldier of the Great War. The Royal Army Service Corps is a splendid regiment without which the army could not function, but not the most romantic in which to serve. The French military authorities have been unable to trace him as having served in the Foreign Legion. It is true that many men changed their names when joining, but this alone would not be in keeping with the vanity of Oswold Atherton Fleming. In September 1911 at the Parish Church in Littlehampton, he had married Winifred Ellen Meyrick, who subsequently divorced him for adultery, the decree being made absolute on June 15, 1925.

At his marriage to Dorothy at Holborn Register Office, he gives his profession as "Journalist"; she, oddly enough, as she was to be the breadwinner for all their married life, lays claim to no profession at all. With a name like Maconochie it is likely that Fleming's mother was Irish; he certainly had the gift of the blarney. Charming, good-looking in a slightly decadent way, he was superficially gifted—a bit of a writer, a bit of a painter, and a very good cook. Perhaps if he had been possessed of more strength of character he would have been an utter rogue. He certainly was not that but rather just a weak "Bonnie Prince Charlie" type, looking for a cushy billet. Women have been taken in by this type of man since the dawn of history, and there is little doubt that, for the first two years at least, Dorothy loved him. She believed all his tales. Like Desdemona, she "loved him for the dangers he had passed," and was sure that one day the right job would turn up for him, that one day his true worth would be appreciated. One day.

Meantime it was Dorothy who provided the home and paid the bills. Oswold left his place in Hammersmith and joined her at Great James Street. Her parents, pleased that she should at last seem "settled," overlooked the Register Office wedding and welcomed "Mac," as he was known, into their midst. They even overlooked his habit of drinking in the pub with the boys instead of going to church. After all, a "war hero" could not be expected to be too conformative in those hectic days. The fiction was kept up for a year or two that he was a journalist "and not always master of his time," as Dorothy wrote when accepting a luncheon invitation. In spite of diligent search I have not been able to find anything published under his name. He is supposed to have been a motoring correspondent for the *News of the World* and to have written a cookery column as "Gourmet" for the *Evening News,* but both these papers disown him. He did produce a cookbook at some time, but it is suspected that his "journalism" may have consisted mostly of propping up well-known Fleet Street bars. In mid-1928 they took more rooms in the Great James Street flat, as Chief Inspector Parker was to do in Great Ormond Street when he married Lady Mary Wimsey.

The carpets are up. The floor is up. . . . The white-washers are washing ceilings as per estimate. The painters are giving two coats of paint as per estimate. . . . The cat is investigating the mysterious cavities between the joists of the flooring, with a view to getting nailed down under the floor if possible.

My husband is giving his celebrated impersonation of the Mayor and Corporation of Ypres surveying the ruins of the Cloth Hall.

I am trying to look like Dido building Carthage, and hoping (as I daresay she did) that the hammering will soon be over.

Life is very wonderful.

Life must have been fairly wonderful from the financial point of view, for not only was she able to enlarge and refurbish the flat, but she bought a cottage at 24 Newland Street, Witham, in Essex, then a quiet market town on the London Road. This was intended as a weekend retreat.

By the end of that year, however, the long honeymoon was over, and something had gone wrong. Dorothy was to remain publicly loyal to Mac for all his life and hers. Nowhere does she complain about him, except in the mildest form when he fails to pass on a message or to re-address a letter. No one is the recipient of her confidences except the public at large, second-hand, through her books. V. S. Naipaul has said, "An autobiography can distort; facts can be realigned. But fiction never lies: it reveals the writer totally." The only way Dorothy could get herself through a crisis was to write it out as fiction, to see it laid down as though it had happened to someone else. It was as if the typewriter were her psychoanalyst or father confessor. Then, when it was all written out, why waste it? Why not publish it? Murder in print the person who had deceived or hurt you. It assuaged the bitterness of her soul and enabled her to forgive and carry on. But she was wrong if she thought it did not show.

There is a rumor that Mac had a child by another woman around this time, and that Dorothy helped the mother financially. I have been unable to verify this fact, but something as catastrophic must have happened. It is quite typical that Dorothy would have assisted the mother. Someone would have had to, and Mac's income scarcely covered his drinks. It may have been that for the first time Dorothy saw him as he really was —a liar, a pretender, a lazy forty-five-year-old schoolboy who would never be her intellectual companion. Although her honesty was such that she could never have married a man whom she did not, or could not in time love, she may also have married him with the hope of providing a father and a home for her own child. This never happened. Although the child later took the name of Fleming, he never lived with them, nor was he legally adopted. Possibly, about this time, Dorothy realized that Mac was unfit to be a father as she saw the father's role, or, as is very likely, Mac refused to have her son anywhere near him.

The outcome of whatever troubled her was *The Documents*

in the Case, the most revealing of her detective books.

It is the only one which does not feature Lord Peter Wimsey, though one character from the Wimsey books, Sir James Lubbock, the Home Office analyst, does appear. It is also the only one in which she acknowledges collaboration. *Busman's Honeymoon,* in which she was joined by Muriel St. Clair Byrne, was originally a play. The only sign of "Robert Eustace's" hand in *The Documents in the Case* is in the medical information, though why she needed to acknowledge assistance for this book and not for *Unnatural Death* and *Have His Carcase* is not clear. "Robert Eustace" was the pen name of Dr. Eustace Robert Barton, M.R.C.S., L.R.C.P., who helped several other writers with medical details, particularly about poisons. Sir Hugh Greene, to whom I am indebted for this information, has traced Dr. Barton's activities from the 1890s to 1947, after which he seems to have completely disappeared. Nowhere is his death recorded—rather appropriate for one who lived so mysteriously.

The Documents in the Case takes the form of letters from the inhabitants of two maisonettes in a Bayswater house to their various friends and relations. *Whose Body?* is also set in Bayswater; no doubt the district's eminent respectability presented the crime writer with a challenge. The upper maisonette is let to two young men, an author and an artist; the lower is occupied by a middle-aged engineer, his bird-brained second wife and a weird companion. (This last character, "Miss Milsom," was a cruel but accurate portrait of a Miss Drennan, an extremely inefficient copy-typist at Benson's.) The story is straightforward, without any of the Wimseyan tangents. The artist falls in love with the silly young wife and the husband is poisoned by the artist with synthetic muscarine, a poison found naturally in a certain kind of fungus. At the insistence of the dead man's adult son certain tests are carried out, and these prove that the poison is artificial and not natural. This and *Busman's Honeymoon* are the only detective books in which Dorothy specifically writes that the murderer was hanged. In most the criminals commit suicide; in yet others the hanging is left to the reader's assumption. Where the Wimsey books abound in named characters running into scores, *Documents* has a mere fifteen, and not only is Wimsey absent—so too, except for a village constable, are the police. It is difficult not to see Harrison, the victim, as Fleming. He was pedantic and pompous, so was Fleming. He dabbled in water colors and crayon drawings, a hobby of Fleming's. He claimed to be an expert cook, so did Fleming. He bullied his wife, and demanded her utmost obedience—Fleming had tried to do this and failed. In this book Dorothy was telling him that he would never succeed; not warning him that she might poison him, that is a bit too fanciful, but showing how his attitude was poisoning their lives.

Harrison was a man of very great sincerity, no imagination and curiously cursed with nerves. It is all wrong for a man of his type to have nerves—nobody believes or understands it. In theory, he was extremely broad-minded, generous and admiringly devoted to his wife; in practice, he was narrow, jealous and nagging. To hear him speak of her, one would have thought him the ideal of chivalrous consideration; to hear him speak to her, one would have thought him a suspicious brute. Her enormous vitality, her inconsequence, her melodrama (that is the real point, I think), got on his nerves, and produced an uncontrollable reaction of irritability. He would have liked her to shine for him and him only; yet a kind of interior shyness prompted him to repress her demonstrations and choke off her confidences. . . . Yet to others he spoke with earnest pride of his wife's brilliance and many-sided intelligence.

It is doubtful if Fleming's shallow mind could take in the lessons she was trying to instill. He may not even have read her books, but at least she unburdened herself, and showed how a marriage could be futilely worn away.

There is a terrible inconsistency in the drawing of the character of the wife. She is described as an empty-headed, pleasure-loving ex-typist, but she writes long, passionate and extremely literate love letters:

When you went away, I felt as if the big frost had got right into my heart. Do you know, it made me laugh when the pipes froze up in the bathroom . . . and He was so angry. I thought if he only knew I was just like that inside, and when the terrible numb feeling had passed off, something would snap in me, too. . . . What right have people to make life such a wasted, frozen thing? Why are they allowed to live at all if they don't *live* in the true sense of the word?

She goes on for pages, even mentioning that she has read *Women in Love*, a difficult book for anyone to get hold of in 1929. "Tyrants make liars," she says. "It is what somebody I read about in the papers calls 'slave-psychology.' I feel myself turning into a cringing slave, lying and crawling to get one little scrap of precious freedom." She discusses sin in a letter of over a thousand words. "No one could commit a sin and be so happy. Sin doesn't exist, the conventional kind of sin, I mean." These passionate letters could not possibly have been penned by a shallow little flirt, but she used the shallow flirt's trick of goading her lover to some kind of action:

I am so frightened. Darling, something dreadful has happened. . . . Do you remember when I said Nature couldn't revenge herself? Oh, but she can and *has*. . . . I've tried things, but it's no good, Petra, you've *got* to help me. I never thought of this—we were so careful—but something must have gone wrong.

Then, when the murder had been done on her behalf, it was all, of course, a false alarm. Another parallel with real life was that Margaret was Harrison's second wife, and was considerably younger than her husband. There was a difference of eleven years between Mac and Dorothy.

It is true that there are dangers in reading too much into an author's work, but *The Documents in the Case* is probably the most self-revealing book among her works. Apart from any disillusions Dorothy may have had over her marriage, 1928 and 1929 were sad years for her. Her father died in the September of 1928 and her mother followed him ten months later. She was attached to both her parents, particularly to her gentle, slightly eccentric father. For her mother's short widowhood Dorothy provided her with a home at Witham, and when she died took her back to Christchurch to be buried with the Reverend Henry. Dorothy had refused to allow solemn hymns at either funeral, and to the astonishment of the villagers raised no head-stone nor memorial to them, so that today their graves are unmarked. In something like shocked outrage the people of Christchurch put up their own plaque inside the church, to their late, beloved rector. This strange action, or rather non-action, of "Miss Dorothy's" is still spoken of in somewhat hushed tones.

Psychoanalysis, science and spiritualism were the "in" things of the twenties and thirties. "Damn the daily papers," says a scientist in *The Documents in the Case.*

And damn education. All these get-clever-quick articles and sixpenny textbooks. Before one has time to verify an experiment, they're all at you, shrieking to have it formulated into a theory. . . . If anybody says there are vitamins in tomatoes, they rush out with a tomato-theory. If somebody says that gamma-rays are found to have an action on cancer-cells in mice, they proclaim gamma-rays as a cure-all for everything from old age to a cold in the head. And if anybody goes quietly away into a corner to experiment with high-voltage electric currents, they start a lot of ill-informed rubbish about splitting the atom.

Another character asks portentously, "What is life?" and gets a most unsatisfactory answer. It seems as though Dorothy was seeking assurance that life was a divine creation, for if it could be invented in the laboratory, where in *that* scheme of things did faith abide?

During the nine years that Dorothy worked at Benson's, she wrote seven full-length Wimsey books, one volume of short stories and *The Documents in the Case.* The average length of each of these books is 275 pages, but this was not all her output. She was a member of the Modern Language Association from 1920, and contributed to the fifth and sixth issues of their journal, *Modern Languages,* with a translation of parts of the Tristan of Thomas. Her full translation was published by Benn in 1929. From 1939 until 1945 she was to be president of the Association. She wrote Wimsey and Montague Egg short stories for *Pearsons, Passing Show,* and other now defunct magazines, and toward the end of the twenties she started to write for broadcasting. After her marriage she gave up the motorcycle and bought a car, a modest affair, nothing like the Daimlers with which she provided Wimsey. Mac claimed to be something of an expert on engines, so he kept it in repair. She used it to visit her parents while they lived, and the child in Westcott Barton.

Dorothy's cousin, Ivy Amy Shrimpton, had come to the then remote village of Westcott Barton in the early twenties and rented Cocksparrow Hall from the lord of the manor. It was a not overlarge Cotswold stone house, standing some way out of the village, which Miss Shrimpton renamed "Sidelings." It had no piped water, sewerage or electricity, but this was not unusual in those days. Miss Shrimpton brought two foster children with her who were not related to each other, the younger one being Dorothy's child. Other children came and went at various times, but these two were fixtures. Miss Shrimpton was hardly ever seen outside the house, but she sent the children regularly to church. She herself was shabby and untidy, and dressed her charges in a strange assortment of garments, cut-down adult clothes from an earlier age. As they never went to school, she must have taught them herself, and cut their hair herself, with blunt shears and a pudding basin if their description is to be believed. They were never allowed to communicate with anyone in the village. Sometimes they went to swing on the garden gate, but would be sharply called in if anyone tried to speak to them. On one occasion, so memorable that it was never forgotten, they were allowed to go to a birthday party. "We are allowed to come," said Dorothy's child, "because you are such a good mother."

There is no evidence whatever that these children, though oddly raised, were in any way ill-treated. Eccentrics and children often get on extremely well together, and the children appear to have been very fond of Miss Shrimpton. One can say, cynically, that there was no one else to be fond of, and children must give affection somewhere; but it would have been very difficult even then to have held growing children against their will if they had suffered physical or mental cruelty. The situation, however, could have been dangerous. These private child-care arrangements, which are illegal nowadays though they do continue, had no official oversight, and the children could have been in a much worse position than the average Poor Law, war orphan, or Dr. Barnado's foster home child. These organizations may at least have seen that their clothing did not make them laughingstocks. Dorothy did visit quite frequently, ostensibly to see Miss Shrimpton, and in spite of herself always came away almost in tears. No one in the village guessed her identity, and although as the child grew older she took more interest in his welfare, sending him eventually to boarding school and Oxford, she never dropped the fiction that she was only an adoptive mother. She supported Miss Shrimpton financially until the latter's death in 1951. Stories were current that the house was found to contain jewelry and cash amounting to £12,000, but this is the kind of tale that always attends the death of any recluse.

One cannot help deploring the tragedy of this situation, the waste of what might have been a rewarding fellowship between mother and child. She longed to be loved, and yet rigidly denied herself one important aspect of love, that of a child for its mother. Her attitude nowadays is difficult to understand when well-known people announce to the world the birth of their illegitimate children in the London *Times,* and the state assists the single mother with her children's upbringing. Fifty years ago people may not have been so broad-minded, but even so the Great War had accustomed them to accept the child born out of wedlock more readily than in Victorian times. It is true that Dorothy was a clergyman's daughter, and it could be thought that her father's parishioners would have disapproved of her conduct, but it would only have been a seven day wonder in East Anglia. Dorothy's strength of character was such that, had she wanted to, she could have outfaced the world with "this is my child, make of it what you will." Had she done this from the start, when she was unknown as a writer, it might have been all right. As time went on and her reputation as a religious apologist grew, such a stance would have been extremely difficult. The great pity is that in her widowhood she was very lonely. A grown-up and married child could have been a solace, but by then they had grown apart, and by the time she died they had not seen each other for several years.

7

The Wimsey Novels

> . . . We are continually tempted to confine the mind of the writer to its expression within his creation, particularly if it suits our purpose to do so. . . . The itch for personally knowing authors torments most of us; we feel that if we could somehow get at the man himself, we should obtain more help and satisfaction from him than from his chosen self-revelation.
>
> Dorothy L. Sayers, *The Mind of the Maker*

"Methinks the lady doth protest too much." Anyone who writes anything at all, whether it be a motto for a Christmas cracker or a ten-part history of the world, means it to be read, and once a thing has been put into print the author must expect to be questioned on it, must expect assumptions to be drawn. If Miss Sayers had written a series of stories about parrots, no one could blame readers for thinking she had once kept a parrot. She would have been deluged with letters from other parrot fanciers asking her advice, pointing out her mistakes, and wanting to know more details about her actual relationship with these birds. Probably she would not have complained, as these questions would have brought forth definite answers. She always, however, complained bitterly when such questions were asked and assumptions made about her Wimsey books, as if they were intrusions into her personal privacy. In effect she would say, "All you need to know is what I have written." If this were so, it would make sterile exercises of all her works. We still know very little about her most intimate thoughts and life, but the few facts which have come to light since her death do illuminate her books, not least her Wimsey stories. It is easy to see now why so many of them had to be written over a comparatively short space of time. With cold calculation she wrote what she knew would sell, but she was too much of a scholar and had too much feeling for her creations to write "cheap thrillers," and whatever she wrote, she could not resist the urge to educate.

The first three Wimsey books were brought out by Ernest Benn Ltd., who had taken them over from Fisher-Unwin. They were dealt with at Benn's by the up and coming, efficient and brilliant Victor Gollancz. Dorothy was not satisfied with the publicity given to her work by Benn's—few authors are ever satisfied with publishers' efforts in this direction—but Dorothy threatened to give up novel-writing altogether. She claims that she was persuaded to continue only because of the great encouragement she received from Gollancz, a highly unlikely story from one who never needed an atom of encouragement to put pen to paper. Gollancz broke from Benn's in 1926, and Dorothy went with him. *Unnatural Death* was already in the presses at Benn's, who were unwilling to let it go, having spent a great deal of money on its preparation. They also had options on Dorothy's next two books. Gollancz needed her name to start off his infant company, but as a man of honor he refused to override Benn's rights. Dorothy, who never ceased to have a grievance against Benn's, had no such qualms but admitted, "I don't actually want a violent row with Benn, because it never pays to make enemies of people, does it? You never know how things may come back on you—and of course, legally the man 'has his rights,' and if he says he paid money for the thing and

I'm now trying to take the thing away, I suppose he has a claim to what he has paid for. I can't do more than ask him to be a sportsman, and perhaps as far as feelings go, he *is* a pachyderm." In the meantime all she could offer Gollancz was a collection of short stories, but she did all she could to inveigle not only writers but even typists from Benn's to Gollancz, frequently embarrassing the almost unabashable Victor. In the end some agreement was arrived at and from 1928 on Gollancz published all her works, save for a few religious tracts and pamphlets which were brought out by Methuen during the war.

Dorothy often pretended that the Wimsey stories were unimportant to her personally, that she wrote them only for amusement, that Wimsey was a purely fictional character, and so on. In reality she took the craft of detective writing extremely seriously. Commenting, in 1925, on an article by Chesterton, she says:

G.K.C. has put his finger at once on the central difficulty of detective fiction—that if you make your solution too obscure and unexpected, the reader is annoyed and says: "Oh, well! that's not fair; nobody could have been expected to guess that." Whereas if you make it too logical and necessary, the reader is again annoyed and says: "Rotten story; I guessed the murderer straight away." It's a most delicate problem of balance, and has only very seldom been solved *perfectly.*

G.K.C. is, of course, a determined upholder of the strictly classic form of the mystery story—not only in theory but in practice, in which point he is superior to Conan Doyle who sometimes departs from the academic ideal. "The thing that we realise must be the thing that we recognise; that is, it must be something previously known, and it ought to be something prominently displayed." That excellent sentence should be illuminated in letters of gold and hung above the desk of every mystery writer. In other words, there should *never* be any clue in the hands of the detective, which is not also in the hands of the reader. Sherlock should never "pick up certain small objects which he placed carefully in an envelope". We must know what the objects are. When the elucidation comes the reader ought to say, in a burst of self-reproach: "Why, of *course!* I ought to have seen that for myself—

it was staring me in the face!" . . . The trouble is, that writers tend, after a time to work to the same formula, so that, after reading half a dozen stories by one man, one begins to see the formula and solve the thing automatically by (a plus b) (a — b).

She goes on:

There is not only a trick but a "craft" of writing mystery stories. It does give just that curious satisfaction which the exercise of cunning crafts-manship always gives to the worker. It is almost as satisfying as working with one's hands. It is rather like laying a mosaic—putting each piece —apparently meaningless and detached—into its place, until one sud-denly sees the thing as a consistent picture. Like mosaic, too, I believe it to be most effective when done in the flat and on rather broad lines.

These were Dorothy's thoughts on detective story writing when she still had only one book in that genre published. The recipient of the letter was John Cournos, one of the mystery men in Dorothy's life. In 1935, over ten years after writing this letter, she gave a lecture at Oxford entitled "Aristotle on Detec-tive Fiction" in which she said:

. . . Your recipe for detective fiction [is] the art of framing lies. From beginning to end of your book, it is your whole aim and object to lead the reader up the garden, to induce him to believe a lie. To believe the real murderer to be innocent, to believe some harmless person to be guilty; to believe the detective to be right where he is wrong and mistaken where he is right; to believe the false alibi to be sound, the present absent, the dead alive and the living dead; to believe in short, anything and everything but the truth.
The art of framing lies—but mark! of framing lies in the *right way*. There is the crux. Any fool can tell a lie, and any fool can believe it; but the right method is to tell the *truth* in such a way that the *intelli-gent* reader is seduced into telling the lie for himself. That the writer himself should tell a flat lie is contrary to all the canons of detective art.

It is in this separation which she made between *detective* fiction for the *intelligent* reader and crime stories for hoi polloi that she has been misunderstood by her critics. If she had an ambition in this line it was to make the mystery story a thing of literary art, something which no don, philosopher or bishop would be ashamed to be found reading—to take, in fact, the plain wrapper off the whodunit. If this was snobbish then she was guilty, but it cannot be denied that she went a great way toward succeeding. Would Maigret have been acceptable if Wimsey had not shown the way?

One can always play games with an author's work, trying to identify the characters with his personal friends, relations, or with well-known public figures. His characters must be based on real people because real people are all he knows. Even when he gives them the bodies and habitats of animals, these animals think and speak like real people. The denizens of outer space in science fiction have to be given some characteristics of mankind, otherwise they would be totally incomprehensible. So, in effect, no one invents a complete character—he will have the looks of this schoolmaster, the mannerisms of that uncle, wear the glaring sweater of a college friend and suffer the heart attack of grandfather, but he will still have to be of a piece. If he is inherently a scholar he is unlikely to mistranslate Latin, or rob a blind man's money box if he is truly a gentleman of breeding; but once created, he belongs to the author. Yet it is difficult to find out who was the inspiration for Wimsey in Dorothy L. Sayers's life. When she started to write about him in *Whose Body?* she was still in love with Eric Whelpton, and Wimsey has some of Whelpton's characteristics—his facility for languages, knowledge of food and appreciation of the good things of life. But physically he was as unlike Whelpton as it was possible to be. This, of course, is one way many authors use to try to avoid identification in their novels. Wimsey was a mere five feet nine, with straw-colored hair, a long face, a beak-like nose, pointed chin, and eyes that were gray in some books, ice blue in others. At the time of his last adventure in *Busman's Honeymoon* he had stretched to just six feet; but by then he had attained his love, Harriet, and love has wondrous effects on a man.

Apart from these slight physical variations Wimsey scarcely alters through thirteen books and fifteen years, in spite of the fact that Dorothy conscientiously adds years to his age. He is supposed to have been born in 1890, which would have made him forty-eight when the last book appeared, a little old for marriage, and almost a pensioner by the time his third son was born, although in the last short story, "Tallboys," he is said to be only fifty-two. Superficially he is a maddening creature. His upper-class mannerisms are awful. There is nothing he cannot do, no trade or hobby with which he does not have at least a nodding acquaintance. He rides superbly, drives like an expert, casts a mighty rod, is a fine cricketer, a dead accurate shot, and a swordsman above the average, can show Valentino a few tricks in bed, play the piano, sing Gospel hymns, etc. etc. ad infinitum. Wimsey does nothing by halves and everything with perfection. His nearest model is, I believe, a character called Adam Adamant who was resurrected for British television a few years ago. And yet, and yet, with all his horrid perfections one cannot help being drawn to the man. He does have a little modesty for himself, even if his creator has none on his behalf. He comes from a family which for fifteen generations has been titled and privileged—very unusual in the English aristocracy; civil wars and revolutions have frequently changed the men at the top. That Dorothy loved this creature she had made is quite obvious. She took great exception, however, to those people who assumed that she and Wimsey were one. In *The Mind of the Maker* she writes:

Well-meaning readers who try to identify the writer with his characters or to excavate the author's personality and opinions from his books are frequently astonished by the ferocious rudeness with which the author himself salutes these efforts at reabsorbing his work into himself. They are an assault upon the independence of his creatures, which he very properly resents. . . . Nor is the offense any more excusable when it takes the form of endowing the creature with qualities . . . which run contrary to the law of its being.

She then quotes a suggestion which was made to her that she allow Lord Peter to end up a convinced Christian:

My dear lady, Peter is not the Ideal Man; he is an eighteenth-century Whig gentleman, born a little out of his time, and doubtful whether any claim to possess a soul is not a rather vulgar piece of presumption.

If Lord Peter Wimsey is *not* the ideal man, the difference after reading the saga from start to finish several times is trivial. Dorothy adds in parenthesis:

(No; you shall not impose either your will or mine upon my creature. He is what he is, I will work no irrelevant miracles upon him, either for propaganda, or to curry favour, or to establish the consistency of my own principles. He exists in his own right and not to please you. Hands off.)

So it is obvious she cared a great deal for Wimsey, who may have represented a long-lost lover or have stood for those moral and ethical values which she considered were vanishing from a civilized world. Was she using the detective story as a long-running modern morality play? Subconsciously perhaps, but the storyteller won over the moralist.

Dorothy's skill is evident when we consider that Wimsey always remains in the forefront of the story even though more intrinsically interesting characters may surround him. Miss Sayers considered that Dickens often made the mistake of swamping his leading characters with minor ones, and it is true that the Dickensian characters we remember best are not the David Copperfields and Oliver Twists but the Micawbers and Fagins. Bunter, Wimsey's ex-batman, now his valet-cum-assistant, could be looked upon as unhealthily devoted to his master, and those books in which he hardly appears do seem to lack something, as if we were waiting for the second half of a double act to appear and not really listening to what the partner, already on stage, is saying. Bunter, who confesses to being one of seven, has a mother who is seventy-five in *Whose Body?* and yet is still alive in *Busman's Honeymoon,* is Wimsey's alter ego. Bunter does all the things it would not be proper for a lord to do, such as worming his way into the hearts of housemaids, flattering charladies and cooks, giving music-hall impersonations and singing vulgar songs—all in the course of duty. He is not, however, obsequious, and does not hesitate to tell off his master should the occasion warrant, in the most courteous way of course. Bunter could have been inspired by Wodehouse's Jeeves, but only insofar as the master/man relationship is concerned. The Wimsey/Bunter partnership is more like that of the medieval knight and squire. Dorothy was fascinated by the King Arthur legend and the whole panoply of chivalry, but there was no money in that when she first began writing. Wimsey is much more a Sir Galahad than an "eighteenth-century Whig gentleman."

Inspector, later Chief Detective Inspector, Parker is deliberately made colorless in comparison; he is described as "nondescript" in *Whose Body?*—a solid workaday policeman who was educated at Barrow-in-Furness Grammar School. Why Barrow-in-Furness? "I do not know that I had any particular reason for placing Parker's childhood there, as I do not know the town at all; I rather felt it to be the kind of industrial place which gave Parker a background as far as possible unlike Peter's, and further than that I can hardly find any good reason for my selection," she wrote to an inquirer in 1936. She is at great pains to emphasize Parker's worthiness (he studies New Testament commentaries when not engaged on police work) and his dull, plodding ways. Such a man was wholly unlikely to have married Wimsey's sister Mary. In *The Mind of the Maker* Dorothy wrote, when discussing the unity of an author's character:

Mr. Micawber is a grand character, instinct with the breath of life; but inefficiency is of his very essence, and it is entirely inconceivable that he should ever have become an efficient detective for the investigation of Mr. Heep's financial frauds. *Somebody* had to detect Heep, and Mr.

Micawber was handy—may indeed have been designed from the out-
set—for the activity; but, superb fun though it all is, we cannot for one
moment believe it.

Nor can *we* believe that the wayward "dropout" Mary would
settle down for a cozy life with a policeman, however high he
rose in the force.

Another impossible marriage is that between Freddy Arbuthnot, a twenties silly-ass type whose only use to Wimsey is that
he knows all about the Stock Exchange, and Rachel Levy, the
daughter of the murdered Jewish financier in *Whose Body?*
Apart from the Dowager Duchess of Denver, modeled on Dorothy's own mother, the rest of the Wimsey clan is uninteresting.
The Duke is a bore, his wife Helen a bitch, and his son, the
Viscount St. George, tiresome. They do not ring true, because
their creator had little personal knowledge of a ducal family in
the twentieth century. It is convenient to make your master
detective a rich lord because he can, with little effort on the
part of the author, do so much more than the modern sleazy
anti-hero sleuths who solve everything with the gun. With
riches anyone can be bribed, or persuaded to talk; with a title
one can get the ear of even the king himself, as in *Clouds of
Witness:*

His next appearance was at the American Embassy. The Ambassador,
however, was not there, having received a royal mandate to dine.
Wimsey damned the dinner . . . and leapt back into his taxi with a
demand to be driven to Buckingham Palace. Here a great deal of
insistence with scandalised officials produced first a higher official, then
a very high official, and, finally, the American Ambassador and a Royal
Personage while the meat was yet in their mouths.
    "Oh, yes," said the Ambassador, "of course it can be done—"
    "Surely, surely," said the Personage genially, "we mustn't have any
delay."

Wimsey was also able to support a kind of unofficial detective
agency staffed entirely by women. The head of this establishment was Miss Climpson,

a thin, middle-aged woman, with a sharp, sallow face and very viva-cious manner. She wore a neat, dark coat and skirt, a high-necked blouse and a long gold neck-chain with a variety of small ornaments dangling from it at intervals, and her iron-grey hair was dressed under a net, in the style fashionable in the reign of the late King Edward.

This description sounds like a portrait of Ivy Compton-Bur-nett, but it is more likely to have been Miss Shrimpton. When Parker, whom Wimsey has naughtily beguiled into believing he is going to be introduced to a light o' love, demands an explana-tion, Wimsey says:

Miss Climpson is a manifestation of the wasteful way in which this country is run. Look at electricity. Look at water-power. Look at the tides. Look at the sun. Millions of power units being given off into space every minute. Thousands of old maids, simply bursting with useful energy, forced by our stupid social system into hydros and hotels and communities and hostels and posts as companions, where their mag-nificent gossip-powers and units of inquisitiveness are allowed to dissi-pate themselves or even become harmful to the community, while the ratepayers' money is spent on getting work for which these women are providentially fitted, inefficiently carried out by ill-equipped police-men like you. My god! it's enough to make a man write to *John Bull*. And then bright young men write nasty little patronising books called "Elderly Women," and "On the Edge of the Explosion"—and the drunkards make songs upon 'em; poor things.

(Unnatural Death)

There has been a resurgence lately in concern about the waste of power, but spinster-power seems to be no longer with us; there just are no spinsters, which is something Dorothy could not possibly have foreseen. Had she done so, she would no doubt have blamed the "break up of the nation" on the disappearance of the single woman. Time and again this specter of the frustrated female comes into the books. Had Dorothy ever known or suffered from such a woman? There were the maiden aunts, Miss Shrimpton, and the Somerville dons, but was the example of any one of these such as to terrify her into a determination, whatever else happened, not to go into old age an inexperienced virgin? It is an open question.

As the Wimsey books are all detective stories, it is not easy to discuss them without giving away their plots. They are all still in print, and there are many people who like their mystery stories to remain mysteries until the end. Dorothy, however, was not always in accord with such people.

I quite appreciate the point you make about the decline of the "pure puzzle" story [she wrote to Gollancz] but I wanted to try my hand at just one of that kind. I am always afraid of getting into a rut, and like each book to have a slightly different idea behind it. I have also been annoyed (stupidly enough) by a lot of reviewers who observed that in *Strong Poison* I had lost my grip because the identity of the murderer was obvious from the start [as indeed it is also in *Unnatural Death* and *The Documents in the Case*].

Personally, I feel that it is only when the identity of the murderer *is* obvious that the reader can really concentrate on the question (much the most interesting), *How* did he do it? But if people really *want* to play "Spot the murderer", I don't mind obliging them—for once!

Each of the books has, as she says, a different idea behind it, other than the detection of murder.

Clouds of Witness (1926), the second Wimsey book, concerns the trial of a peer for murder, and gives a good description of a now obsolete ceremony. The right of a peer to be tried by his peers was abolished later, and probably because of this the book seems much more old-fashioned than its date would suggest, even though one is surprised to find that *The Times* could be delivered by air daily from London to Paris—in time for breakfast, too—as long ago as the early twenties. The Wimseys, it is said, belonged to the kind of society where cheating at cards "was regarded as far more shameful than such sins as murder and adultery." Dorothy's high society must have been different from Evelyn Waugh's. We hear a lot about "them dirty Russians as wants to blow us all to smithereens" and there is a great foreshadowing of women's lib; when the Dowager suggests that her daughter's penniless lover would be insulted with the suggestion that he should live on his mother-in-law, Mary replies, "Why not? George doesn't believe in those old-fashioned ideas about property. Besides, if you'd given it to me, it would be *my* money. We believe in men and women being equal. Why should the one always be the breadwinner more than the other?" This was written before Dorothy married Fleming, when she did not know that her fate *was* to be the breadwinner. In her later books there is a hankering for the old established order of things, although when Wimsey eventually marries Harriet there is no suggestion that she should give up her profession in subservience to her lord.

Clouds of Witness embodies all those things which made critics so furious with Dorothy L. Sayers. Firstly, her snobbery —the whole clue to the mystery is contained in a letter in French which is read to the lords without translation, the assumption being that all members of the upper house were fluent in the language. There is a translation in the book, but one feels it is only there at the publisher's insistence. Then too, there are the painfully long lead-ups to clues:

Lord Peter suddenly bundled out of bed with a violent jerk and sped across the landing to the bathroom.

Here he revived sufficiently to lift up his voice in "Come unto these Yellow Sands." Thence, feeling in a Purcellish mood, he passed to "I attempt from Love's Fever to Fly," with such improvement of spirits that, against all custom, he ran several gallons of cold water into the bath and sponged himself vigorously. Wherefore, after a rough towelling, he burst explosively from the bathroom, and caught his shin somewhat violently against the lid of a large oak chest which stood at the head of the staircase. . . .

Within this oak chest lay the clue, and all that was needed to help the story along was for Peter to bang his shin against it.

Nor does Peter play absolutely fair with the truth, truth which Dorothy always maintained should be inviolate. He lies to the police about Grimethorpe: "He has an unfortunate grudge against my brother. In connection with a poaching matter—up in Yorkshire." Thus the public reputation of Denver is saved, and no doubt it could be maintained that stealing a man's wife is as much poaching as stealing his pheasants.

Clouds of Witness was followed a year later by *Unnatural Death,* and in 1928 by *The Unpleasantness at the Bellona Club.*

This last-named book does more to invoke the disillusion of the twenties than any social tract could do—the disillusion of soldiers who were not killed in battle in the First World War but instead sentenced to a slow death over years through unemployment and the forgetting of promises of a "land fit for heroes," coupled with the hypocrisy, as it seems now, of Armistice Day. Then there were the charlatans, who were difficult to distinguish from the real men of ideas. Rejuvenation was a great talking point, particularly through the use of glandular extracts. Any elderly active man such as George Bernard Shaw was rumored to have been given a new lease of life by means of "glands." Everyone took them up, including Mrs. Rushworth in this book.

"Are you devoted to young criminals by any chance? Wimsey said that they presented a very perplexing problem."

"How very true. So perplexing. And just to think that we have been quite wrong about them all these thousands of years. Flogging and bread and water, you know, and Holy Communion, when what they really needed was a little bit of rabbit gland or something to make them just as good as gold. . . . And all those poor freaks in side-shows too—dwarfs and giants you know—all pineal and pituitary, and they come right again. Though I daresay they make a great deal more money as they are, which throws such a distressing light on unemployment, does it not?"

Wimsey said that everything had the defects of its qualities.

The Unpleasantness at the Bellona Club is, in my opinion, one of the best Wimsey books, chiefly because it is straightforward in the telling. It does not go off into side issues, nor is it tainted with the worst of Dorothy's prejudices. It also contains some wildly comic "Bloomsbury" dialogue.

The next book in the series is *Strong Poison,* in which we first meet Harriet Vane, with whom Wimsey falls in love. "Though on the whole," Dorothy writes:

I do not care for love-interest in a detective story, there is a great deal in what he [Chesterton] says about its usefulness as camouflage. In fact, I think the reason why it is so seldom successful is because it is unnecessarily foisted into a story which would be complete without it—as in those sentimental intrusions which I deprecate (and skip) in Austin Freeman's otherwise admirable work. In the stories in which it is successful it forms an integral part of the plot, as in that incomparable classic *The Moonstone,* where the whole story revolves about the love of two dissimilar (but both admirably drawn) women for Franklin Blake. Bentley has used it well also in *Trent's Last Case*—the matrimonial relations of Mr. and Mrs. Manderson (very restrained and good), the splendidly managed red herring of the supposed intrigue between Mrs. Manderson and Marlowe—and Trent's own love for Mrs. M. which prevents him from accusing Marlowe, and provides a plausible *cheville* to connect the two parts of the story.

What made Dorothy suddenly bring love into the Wimsey stories is not known; it may be that it just fell in as the story went along. There is no doubt that Harriet is Dorothy as she saw herself. She could not imagine anyone else falling in love with Wimsey. It may also be that she was far enough away from events in her own life to see them in perspective. Harriet resembles Dorothy in looks, being tall and dark-haired, not by any means beautiful. She had "a nice throat" with "a kind of arum lily quality." She wrote detective stories, and always signed her name Harriet *D.* Vane, an echo of Dorothy's insistence on her "L." Like Dorothy she had a beautiful speaking voice. She refuses Wimsey's offers of marriage all through *Strong Poison* and *Have His Carcase,* finally succumbing at the end of *Gaudy Night.* She does not appear at all in *Five Red*

Herrings, Murder Must Advertise or *The Nine Tailors,* and in all
these books a love interest on Wimsey's part would have been
intrusive. The reason Harriet kept him dangling for so long was,
firstly, because she felt under an obligation to him, as indeed she
was, for her very life; and gratitude is no basis for a good marriage. Secondly, she had been deeply scarred, and not only by
her trial on a charge of murdering her lover. This man, who had
professed to be "conscientiously opposed to any formal marriage," had badgered her to form "an irregular liaison with
him." After much struggling with her principles she had consented, and they had set up house together. After a year he
proposed marriage, an action which had so enraged Harriet she
walked out on him. She was angry with Boyes because, after
persuading her against her will to adopt his principles of conduct, he then renounced those principles and so, as she says
"made a fool" of her. She tells Wimsey:

Philip . . . wanted devotion. I gave him that. I did, you know. But I
couldn't stand being made a fool of. I couldn't stand being on proba-
tion, like an office-boy, to see if I was good enough to be conde-
scended to. I quite thought he was honest when he said he didn't
believe in marriage—and then it turned out that it was a test, to see
whether my devotion was abject enough. Well, it wasn't. I didn't like
matrimony offered as a bad-conduct prize.

This may sound convoluted—but it has the ring of bitterly
experienced truth; and in a way it is a pity that the story did not
stay in that groove—but Dorothy was quite unable to keep any
of her works in grooves. The book ranges over false mediums
—a topical subject of the time—the properties of arsenic and
the science of lock picking. It introduces a gospel-singing re-
formed burglar straight out of *Major Barbara.* Was Dorothy
mocking other mystery writers when she twice mentions that,
on being handed a sheet of typescript, Wimsey noticed "me-
chanically . . . that it was typed on a Woodstock machine, with
a chipped lower case p, and a capital A that was out of align-

ment"? She herself always made fun of this sort of thing. It is in this book that Wimsey says, "in detective stories virtue is always triumphant. They're the purest literature we have."

Five Red Herrings was set in and around Kirkcudbright, and was, as Dorothy says, "a plot invented to fit a real locality." For several years she and Mac spent their holidays there in September, at 14a High Street. An uncle of Dorothy's built boats over at the Stell, and two maiden aunts also lived in the town. Maiden aunts seem so prolific in her family it is no wonder she was anxious to marry, but of course they may have been the same aunts popping up in different places. *Five Red Herrings* seems to me not the best Wimsey book, and I find it commits the unpardonable sin in a detective work of being exceedingly dull. It has also dated, I believe, more than any of the others. It was obviously written to please the people of Kirkcudbright, among whom she was very happy. A lady still living in the town has sent me this description of her:

She appeared to be middle aged, with her hair greyish, cut in a no-nonsense sort of fashion, scraped back from her round moon face. She wore a peculiar sort of outfit, consisting of a black hat, wide brimmed, shallow crowned, it looked and probably was an old fashioned parson's hat such as Church of England vicars wore in the days of my distant youth. A rather long black coat, slightly waisted, a broad figure she had, with rather thick ankles which were clad in greyish hand knitted stockings and clumping brogues on her feet. She usually carried a long black stick with a big flat silver knob on its top. Her voice was rather loud and she seemed to chat a lot. I remember being at a furniture sale when Dorothy Sayers bought a piece of old pewter communion plate for the then big price of £15. Her husband was said to compile cookery books. Her presence did not attract much attention in the town for after all we had well-known people living there all the time. To be quite candid I thought she did not look at all brainy, but a little stupid as though she might be a bit dull, though scraps of her conversation, overheard because of her penetrating voice gave the lie to this impression.

Five Red Herrings gave Dorothy quite a bit of trouble; even finding the title, at which she was usually so good, kept eluding her, as she wrote to Gollancz in September 1930:

The nuisance is that I can't hit on a good title. As you know, I wanted to call it "The Six Suspects", but somebody has pinched that. I might call it:

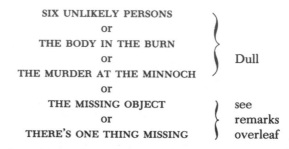

SIX UNLIKELY PERSONS	
or	
THE BODY IN THE BURN	Dull
or	
THE MURDER AT THE MINNOCH	
or	
THE MISSING OBJECT	see
or	remarks
THERE'S ONE THING MISSING	overleaf

or I may think of something really good and suitable as I go on. I've thought of one little stunt to add spice to the business. When the body is found, Lord Peter and the police catalogue all the contents of the pockets, etc., etc., and Lord Peter says to Sergeant Dalziel:

"There's something missing. Look everywhere for it. If we can't find it, it means Murder."

The Sergeant not unnaturally asks what he is to look for, and Wimsey tells him, but actually the Sergeant and the reader, if he had understood enough about the dead man's occupation in life, ought to have been able to supply for himself the name of the missing object from the list of things which *were* there.

Now, what I propose to do is to leave out altogether the paragraph in which Wimsey describes the missing object and the reasons why he knows it is missing, and substitute a blank page, in which the reader is invited to use his wits.

As the story goes on, six suspects appear, against whom the evidence (as regards motive, means, opportunity etc.) is practically equal. About the penultimate chapter, various members of the police give their opinions—one saying he thinks A is the murderer, another plumping for B, the third for C and so on. Wimsey says "You are all very plausible, but it was B and as a matter of fact *I know* this"—his reason being that he has discovered which of them has the missing object. The reader will know which of them has it, provided, of course, that he has previously made up his mind what the missing object is. Wimsey then reconstructs the crime, ingeniously destroying the most convincing alibi of the whole six, and the murderer is arrested and confesses.

The missing paragraph can be printed, if desired, in a sealed page at the end of the book, or it may merely be supplied by Wimsey in conversation in the final chapter.

Do you like this idea?

No, Gollancz did not like the idea. The book, however, sold well and the next year she wrote of visitors to Kirkcudbright "yelping for copies and hastening in cars and charabancs to view the place where the Body was found." She complains that Gollancz's salesman has not seen that any copies were available in the town "and when I am on the spot ready to autograph books. Too, *too* sickmaking!"

Harriet reappears in *Have His Carcase* (1932). Having realized that "The best remedy for a bruised heart is not, as so many people seem to think, repose upon a manly bosom. Much more efficacious are honest work, physical activity, and the sudden acquisition of wealth," she goes on a walking tour, and being the accident-prone young woman that she is, finds the body.

Michael Innes tells a story of how the B.B.C. commissioned four detective writers to collaborate on a series, three men and Dorothy. The first man wanted the story to begin with four bridge players in a room with a heavy velvet curtain over the window. During the game they were so absorbed they did not notice blood trickling from behind the curtain and eventually engulfing the card table. The second writer said this was silly as blood did not flow like this, it clotted. Unless, said a third writer, "the victim was a hemophiliac." Miss Sayers said nothing but jotted something in her notebook. Her next bestseller was about a murdered hemophiliac.

Well, yes, perhaps that may have been the springboard for *Have His Carcase,* except that the B.B.C. serial was commissioned in 1930, before *Strong Poison* and *Five Red Herrings* appeared. It was called "Behind the Screen," and the other participants were Hugh Walpole, F. C. Bentley, Ronald Knox, Valentine Williams and Agatha Christie. Michael Innes cites Ronald Knox as the source of his story.

A much more likely inspiration for *Have His Carcase* was John Cournos. He was undoubtedly a very great friend of Dorothy's, possibly a lover; but if so, it would have been before 1924, when he married Sybil Norton. He was born in Kiev in 1881 and emigrated with his family to Philadelphia when he was ten. He knew no English then, and indeed was quite illiterate in any language, as he had never been to school in Russia. His was a typical emigrant's tale. Starting as a newsboy, he taught himself to read from the papers he delivered, and ended up as assistant editor of the *Philadelphia Record.* He came to England in 1912 and joined Gordon Craig's theater school committee. During the First World War he was employed at Marconi House, decoding Russian government messages. In 1917 he joined the Foreign Office, was a member of the Anglo-Russian Commission to Petrograd, and was marooned there during the bloodiest days of the Revolution. Returning to England he joined the political intelligence department of the Foreign Office, but resigned in 1920 to become a full-time writer. He served several months as an investigator of the famine areas for the Save the Children Fund. His published works occupy nearly two columns of the reference books. Music was his chief passion apart from literature. Before the Second World War he returned to America, and died there in 1966.

Cournos, if anyone, was the prototype of Wimsey, and most certainly he would have provided the medical and technical details for *Have His Carcase,* as well as the arsenic theory in *Strong Poison.* The monk Rasputin was alleged to have made himself immune to poison by continually taking small doses of it. It has proved difficult to find out much more about Cournos than is revealed in the reference books; his *Autobiography*, written in 1935, is no longer obtainable in the United Kingdom. He may have been responsible for Dorothy's anti-Soviet bias, either because he was rabidly for or against the Soviet Union. The most revealing of his titles is *London under the Bolsheviks*, published by the Russian Liberation Committee, 1919, which seems to suggest he was against.

What he certainly would have provided for *Have His Carcase* was the Playfair cipher, the working out of which occupies seven boring pages if one is not cryptically inclined. The book loses nothing, however, by skipping these pages entirely—an example of Dorothy's efforts to please all the people all the time. But she does cheat a bit; the mystery is never completely cleared up. For example, we do not learn who posted the Czechoslovakian letters—from Warsaw! Or why the murderers had to go through such tortuous methods of doing away with the victim. The "point of medicine" on which the plot turns is quite obvious from the start today. We are much better medically informed, and the "curse of the Romanoffs" has been featured in many films and books since *Have His Carcase* was published. We know immediately the chap had hemophilia, and it is irritating to have to plow through nearly three hundred pages before Wimsey and Co. catch up. There is a highly unlikely scene in a theatrical agent's office, and another in a hospital. Where on earth did Miss Sayers get the idea that hospital nurses always called their patients by numbers? It happens in this book, and in *Gaudy Night*. As one who bounced with what can only be called rude health, her experience of hospitals was limited. Did they do it, I wonder, in the Bournemouth nursing home to protect the identity of their patients? It is possible, but cannot be checked now as the place has long ceased to be a nursing home. For one who always prided herself on the precision of her information she makes quite a few odd slips.

The book for which Dorothy is supposed to have done the

most meticulous research is *The Nine Tailors*. She happened to be wandering around a secondhand bookshop when she picked up for sixpence a little book called *Change Ringing* by C. A. W. Troyte. The thing fascinated her as the Playfair ciphers had done, and she worked over it until she could write out on paper a complete touch of Grandsire Triples or Kent Treble Bob Majors. It was the words in the first place which attracted her, then the beauty of the mathematics, and finally she saw in it a way of hiding clues—the story came later. Dorothy started on a book involving bell ringing in 1932, but had to put it aside for lack of technical details. To meet her obligations to Gollancz she wrote, somewhat hurriedly, *Murder Must Advertise*. One subject she knew from A to Z was advertising, and if she had not tried so hard to make the story topical and full of incident, I think this book would be one of her best. Anyone who ever worked in an office in the thirties cannot fail to be transported back to those days, so exactly do the scenes set in Messrs. Pyms recall the chatter, the scandal, the tea drinking, the long intervals when the typists had nothing to do but file their nails which culminated in hectic flourishes of work, the paternal employer, and that vanished race, messenger boys. London in the thirties was full of them—boys in pillbox caps and silver-buttoned "bum-freezers," telegram boys, and gorgeously appareled hotel pages—even the B.B.C. had a long, sober-suited line of scrubbed young lads. The boys vanished with the Second World War, and with the raising of the school-leaving age and the growth of electronic communications they were never replaced—but whatever happened to all those uniforms? If the whistling lads are no longer with us, advertising itself has scarcely changed. Not so long ago in England there used to be a television commercial for margarine which employed the phrase "anyone can keep a cow in the kitchen." Pym's produced: "If you kept a cow in the kitchen you could get no better bread spread than G. P. Margarine." Dorothy had great fun inventing what she thought were outrageous products. "They're putting out a tinned porridge, 'Piper Parritch.' No boiling, no stirring—only heat the tin. Look for the Piper on the label."

You can buy tinned anything nowadays, including porridge —and we are still bothered by the advertiser's impertinent and personal questions: "Mother! has your child learned regular habits?"; "Are you *sure* that your toilet paper is germ-free?"; "Your most intimate friends dare not ask you this question"; "Do you suffer from superfluous hair?"; "Do you ever ask yourself about body odor?"

Wimsey, disguised as trainee copywriter Death Bredon, toiled over Sanfect—"Wherever there's Dirt, there's Danger!"; "The Skeleton in the Water-Closet." There is a description of do-it-yourself furniture:

You can sit on a Darling chair, built up in shilling and sixpenny sections and pegged with patent pegs at sixpence a hundred. If Uncle George breaks the leg you buy a new leg and peg it in. If you buy more clothes than will go into your Darling chest of drawers, you unpeg the top, purchase a new drawer for half a crown, peg it on and replace the top.

This book is an encouraging reminder that life does not move at an ever-accelerating rate and that the old adage "there is nothing new under the sun" holds good. Unfortunately it is very nearly spoiled by a terrific amount of nonsense. Wimsey, who must by now be all of forty-three, goes cavorting around the countryside in a harlequin costume, diving into a fountain: ". . . The slim body shot down through the spray, struck the surface with scarcely a splash and slid through the water like a fish." He lures a fast woman with a pennywhistle and she, poor soul, suffers a terrifying moment of E.S.P. or, as might be said today, "a bad trip":

I'm seeing something I can't make out. I've got it now. Straps. They are strapping his elbows and dropping a white bag over his head. The hanged man. There's a hanged man in your thoughts. Why are you thinking of hanging?

And there are eleven pages entirely devoted to a cricket match, all to prove that Tallboy could hit any object he aimed at.

"The new book is nearly done," Dorothy wrote from Kirkcudbright in September, 1932.

I hate it, because it isn't the one I wanted to write, but I had to shove it in because I couldn't get the technical dope on *The Nine Tailors* in time. Still, you never know what the public will fancy, do you? It will tell people a little about the technical side of advertising, which most people are inquisitive about, and it deals with dope traffic, which is fashionable at the moment, but I don't feel that this part is convincing, as I can't say I "know dope". Not one of my best efforts. The "Nine Tailors" will be a labour of love—and probably be a FLOP!!

The Nine Tailors was anything but a flop, though pedants have found errors in the campanology. So infuriated was a Mr. Willie Roughton as late as 1947 that he refused to cooperate with the B.B.C. in a program, "Bells of London," because they used a quotation from *The Nine Tailors*. "I am quite sure Miss Sayers had not been in a belfry when she wrote her book," he said. And he was quite right, as Dorothy told the *Star*, "of *course* I know nothing about bell-ringing." It really does not detract from the book if she wrote "double dodge in 7–8" instead of "triple dodge in 78" and "slow hunt" instead of "slow work." Where she should say "treble bob hunting" she writes, "Sabaoth, released from the monotony of the slow hunt, ran out merrily into her plain hunting course." But that *sounds* much better in words, and keeps the rhythm of the paragraph. The real glaring error is that she allows the rector to relieve the ringers at various times. This is absolutely not allowed. Once a peal has begun it has to be completed by the same team. It is doubtful if poor old Hezekiah Lavender could possibly have rung Tailor Paul, weighing forty-one hundredweight, for nine hours; but these are minor errors when one takes into account that it was all worked out on paper.

It was not until 1936 that Dorothy actually saw peals being rung, at the dedication of a ring of twelve in Croydon. "I went up to the bell-chamber where, I am happy to say, I did not drop dead—but I certainly should not have cared for nine hours of it at close quarters!" This leads to another dubious point. Medical men are of the opinion that no one could actually be killed by a loud noise. The man would probably have been deafened early in the ring and made giddy by the vibrations, but death was unlikely except, of course, from sheer fright. The effect of the bells on Wimsey is considered to be impossible, but for campanologists to make such a fuss as they still do is just quibbling. After all, the naturalists do not complain about her "shrieking bat" or "moth's tooth," and she did arouse a great deal of interest in the science of bell-ringing—indeed, she brought the word "campanology" into common usage.

Fenchurch St. Paul is a mixture of the Upwell, March and Walpole St. Peter churches, various features taken from each. The Reverend Theodore Venables is a lifelike portrait of her father—although the Reverend Henry was not a bell-fancier, not having the opportunity in his meager red brick church. It is an affectionate portrait of a scholarly, generous, slightly eccentric man. Christchurch people today claim that they can recognize almost all the village characters. The description of the Fens and the "drown" are truly evocative; the only jarring note is the clockwork precision of the emergency arrangements. This, no doubt, was how it was *meant* to be, but not how it was likely to go. The rushing out of the waters was usually far too sudden to bring into action even the best-laid battle plan. The police methods seem a bit dubious; and was it really possible in 1933 to catch suspects by bugging them with microphones? The story goes along at a cracking pace, and the book was, deservedly, a runaway best-seller. It was a Book Society recommendation in England, very rare for a detective novel, but they considered it "not only a brilliant detective novel—it is also a brilliant straight novel"—a little condescending perhaps. Incidentally, modern writers who sometimes have to wait months to see their works in print may envy the speed of production in the thirties. On August 30, 1933, Dorothy was telling Gollancz she had reached an awkward point in *The Nine Tailors*. On January 8, 1934, the book was published.

If I think *The Nine Tailors* was Dorothy's best book, I find its successor, *Gaudy Night*, certainly her worst. It has quite a good idea behind it, the tracing of a poison pen writer in a women's college—the revenge theme. There are some splendid characters, and some very good isolated scenes. Dorothy herself called it "an overgrown monster," as it is nearly 350 pages long, and adds:

It is the only book I have written which embodies any kind of "moral" and I do feel rather passionately about this business of the integrity of the mind—but there it is—it's the book I wanted to write and I have written it. . . . I wouldn't claim that it was in itself a great work of great literary importance; it is important to me.

The "integrity of the mind"—but was she exercising that integrity to use the format of a detective novel to preach a sermon? Here was a captive, and captivated, audience, already in love with her characters, and wham! they are hit over the head with a treatise on ultimate truth. There is not even a corpse! Dorothy might have argued that truth should be proclaimed everywhere, and by any means, but her readership felt cheated. That was not likely to encourage people in the search for truth. Along with this theme is Dorothy's perennial highlighting of the damage which can be done by sexually frustrated females. In an "Author's note" she affirms emphatically that "none of the characters which I have placed upon this public stage has any counterpart in real life. In particular, Shrewsbury

College, with its dons, students and scouts, is entirely imaginary." Somerville did not think so; it took them years to forgive
her and even today she is not the most beloved of their alum-
nae. What chiefly annoyed them, apart from the supposition
that a women's college was perforce a hotbed of neurotics, was
that the college she depicted in 1935 was no different from the
one she had known in 1912. Somerville considered that it had
not only moved with the times, but gone ahead of them. The
book begins with a Gaudy, that is, an old students' reunion. One
fault in the book is Dorothy's assumption that *everyone* knows
how a college in a university works, and she gives no explana-
tion either of the term "Gaudy Night" itself, or of how a college
is run. The vast number of people who read detective novels in
the thirties would not be aware of what was a warden, what a
dean and so on. If they persevered with the book they would
probably have picked up a little, but it did need perseverance.
The assembling of the ex-students gave Dorothy a chance to
sketch in a whole lot of highly recognizable characters and to
take revenge on a few of them. There was Miss Mollison, who
would insist on telling Harriet Vane a long tale which she was
quite sure would make a splendid detective story—every writer
has suffered this kind of affliction. The appalling American, Miss
Schuster-Slatt, with her crusade for the sterilization of the unfit,
is a bit overdrawn, but there were a number of similar Americans about at that time:

Miss Schuster-Slatt said she thought English husbands were lovely, and
that she was preparing a questionnaire to be circulated to the young
men of the United Kingdom, with a view to finding out their matrimonial preferences.

Shades of Kinsey!
    There is Miss Barton, who throughout the book acts as a kind
of conscience. She questions the whole moral aspect of writing
detective stories.

"Well," said Harriet ". . . writers can't pick and choose until they've made money. If you've made your name for one kind of book and then switch over to another, your sales are apt to go down, and that's the brutal fact." She paused. "I know what you're thinking—that anybody with proper sensitive feeling would rather scrub floors for a living. But I should scrub floors very badly, and I write detective stories rather well." . . .

"But surely," persisted Miss Barton, "you must feel that terrible crimes and the sufferings of innocent suspects ought to be taken seriously, and not just made into an intellectual game."

"I do take them seriously in real life. Everybody must. But should you say that anybody who had tragic experience of sex, for example, should never write an artificial drawing-room comedy?"

"But isn't that different?" said Miss Barton, frowning. "There is a lighter side to love; whereas there's no lighter side to murder."

That Dorothy did have qualms about making money out of crime is evident throughout her work. One part of her was uneasy about profiting from evil, even if the evil was only of the fictional kind. In November 1935 she spoke at the Oxford Union in support of the motion "That the present excessive indulgence in the solution of fictitious crime augurs ill for our national future." As the Oxford Union does not appear to keep any records I have not been able to find out what exactly she said.

Among the ex-students of Dorothy's Shrewsbury is Catherine Bendick, née Freemantle, a rather catty portrait of Doreen Wallace. Doreen, who had, in 1922, married a well-known Suffolk farmer, Rowland Rash, became involved in agitation for the abolition of tithes. In the days of the great agricultural depression many farmers were being made bankrupt and their farms and stock sold because they could not, or would not, pay the church dues. The ecclesiastical authorities behaved, to say the least, with consummate stupidity. Dorothy, a clergyman's daughter, was naturally in favor of the continued payment of these charges. She had, as she said, "been educated by the tithes." In *The Nine Tailors* the rector says:

Not that we have had any trouble about tithe in this parish. Our farmers are very sensible. A man from St. Peter came to talk to me about it, but I pointed out to him that the 1918 adjustment was made in the farmers' interests and that if they thought they had reason to complain of the 1925 Act, then they should see about getting a fresh adjustment made. But the law, I said, is the law. Oh, on the matter of tithe I assure you I am adamant. Adamant.

This is not the place to argue the rights and wrongs of the tithes, but the reverend gentleman was talking nonsense. In Dorothy's eyes the law *was* the law—inviolate until it was changed. Doreen pointed out that every backward movement had been made by the law keepers, every tyrant had claimed to be upholding the law, every step forward had been made by the law breakers, even, she flung at Dorothy at the end of a sizzling correspondence, your precious Jesus Christ. Doreen could not understand how anyone with so clear and logical mind as Dorothy's could maintain the illogical stance of a church supported by one section of the community. Did Dorothy pay the church one tenth of her income from her books? Back and forth flew the letters, until, horror of horrors, from her seat in the cinema Dorothy saw on the newsreel her old Somerville crony bawling from a farm wagon in Hyde Park! All communication between them ceased entirely from then on. Catherine Bendick in *Gaudy Night* is depicted as a down-trodden, work-worn woman, "a Derby winner making shift with a coal-cart." It was unkind and very untrue. Doreen had managed to support the farm, and the anti-tithe agitation, by writing several best-selling novels, which Dorothy considered as using her gifts for the wrong purpose.

Far from being imaginary, most of the characters assembled for the Gaudy could be recognized by someone. "The bony woman with the long horse-face who had devoted herself to Settlement work" appeared in my own life many years later as Lettice Jowitt. "She always seemed such a *silly* woman," Let-

tice said of Dorothy, "always talking rubbish in that loud voice
—very deceptive—she had a marvellous brain."

The book is mostly a series of conversations, discussions on
the nature of truth. The whole book may have been sparked off
by C. P. Snow's then recently published *The Search*, which is
discussed in the Common Room at Shrewsbury.

"It's about a man who starts out to be a scientist and gets on very well
till, just as he's going to be appointed to an important executive post,
he finds he's made a careless error in a scientific paper. . . . Somebody
finds out, and he doesn't get the job. So he decides he doesn't really
care about science after all." . . .

"The point about it," said Wimsey, "is what an elderly scientist says
to him. He tells him: 'The only ethical principle which has made
science possible is that the truth shall be told all the time. If we do not
penalize false statements made in error, we open up the way for false
statements by intention. . . .' "

The ethical question in *Gaudy Night* is whether a man should
have been penalized for withholding information which he
knew would have invalidated a thesis he was presenting. The
man was brilliant, the piece of information esoteric. Should he
have been lost to scholarship for this minor lie? The discussions
go on interminably with, intermittently, a flurry into detection
as if Miss Sayers had suddenly remembered what kind of book
she was supposed to be writing. It does have one or two high
spots of comedy—particularly the account of a literary party.
The description of the plot of the Book of the Moment's Choice
makes one long to read the complete novel. No one at the party
had read *Mock Turtle* except:

. . . a young man . . . said he had read it and thought it rather interesting,
only a bit long. It was about a swimming instructor at a watering-place,
who had contracted such an unfortunate anti-nudity complex through
watching so many bathing-beauties that it completely inhibited all his
natural emotions. So he got a job on a whaler and fell in love at first
sight with an Eskimo, because she was such a beautiful bundle of
garments. So he married her and brought her back to live in a suburb,
where she fell in love with a vegetarian nudist. So then the husband

went slightly mad and contracted a complex about giant turtles, and spent all his spare time staring into the turtle-tank at the Aquarium . . . it was one of those books that reflect the author's reactions to Things in General. Altogether, significant was, he thought, the word to describe it.

Perhaps one day someone will write it.

The learned discussion at High Table as to why dress shirts go "pop" is also very funny.

Most of the investigating of the mystery is left to Harriet, with Wimsey bobbing in and out between important Foreign Office assignments. There is some ridiculous business of a dog collar, and some quite gratuitous violence regarding a chess set. The villain, as in *Unnatural Death*, is a woman, but like Margaret in *The Documents in the Case*, she behaves far too intelligently for the kind of woman she is supposed to be. She would never, had she not understood the words, have been able to understand the significance of the Latin extract pinned to a dummy in a scholar's gown. (Nor do non-classicists, for Miss Sayers does not deign to translate.)

The best thing about the book is that at last Harriet consents to marry Wimsey. She realized on a trip up the river that it would have to be:

. . . she studied his half-averted face. Considered generally, as a façade, it was by this time tolerably familiar to her, but now she saw details, magnified as it were by some glass in her own mind. The flat setting and fine scroll-work of the ear, and the height of the skull above it. The glitter of close-cropped hair where the neck-muscles lifted to meet the head. A minute sickle-shaped scar on the left temple. The faint laughter-lines at the corner of the eye and the droop of the lid at its outer end. The gleam of gold down on the cheek-bone. The wide spring of the nostril. An almost imperceptible beading of sweat on the upper lip and a tiny muscle that twitched the sensitive corner of the mouth. The slight sun-reddening of the fair skin and its sudden whiteness below the base of the throat. The little hollow above the points of the collar-bone.

He looked up; and she was instantly scarlet, as though she had been dipped in boiling water. . . . Then the mist cleared. His eyes were riveted upon the manuscript again, but he breathed as though he had been running.

That woman, whoever she was, certainly loved that man, whoever he was.

8

Wimsey Nears His End

Oh, Peter . . . All my life I have been wandering in the dark
—but now I have found your heart—and am satisfied.

And what do all the great words come to in the end, but
that?—I love you—I am at rest with you—I have come
home.

Dorothy L. Sayers, *Busman's Honeymoon*

It is probable that *Gaudy Night* was intended to be the last of
the Wimsey saga. There are references back in the text to almost all the other books, which looks as if Dorothy was drawing
all the threads together preparatory to a final launching. She
may have thought that marrying Wimsey off was a sure way of
getting rid of what she was coming to believe was an incubus.
She was, as the questionings in *Gaudy Night* show, becoming
more and more conscience-stricken about the ethical aspect of
detective writing, and she was not absolutely sure that someone
at some time might not get an idea for murder from one of her
books. These were, however, surface qualms; if she had felt very
deeply about it she could have withdrawn all the works from
circulation. More fundamental to the matter was that she was
genuinely tired of the characters and running short of ideas.
Nearly all the Wimsey books and the short stories spring out of

items featured in the news at the time, or, as in the case of *Gaudy Night,* from a book by another author.

However, if *Gaudy Night* was meant to be Wimsey's swan song, she also no doubt kept him in reserve, to resurrect whenever funds looked like running low. At that moment there were other things she wanted to do; one was to write a life of Wilkie Collins, and that "straight" novel, too, was always thudding at the back of her mind. Dorothy felt she had come to a crossroads, but was not quite sure which turning to take. It was Muriel St. Clare Byrne who suggested she should try writing for the stage. Miss Byrne had come to Somerville in 1914, at the beginning of Dorothy's final year, and they had met again at the first M.A. ceremony in 1920. With Helen Simpson and Marjorie Barber she formed with Dorothy a quartet of like minds. They frequently met to dine and talk interminably. Miss Byrne was a specialist of the Tudor period and the author of several books dealing with various aspects of Elizabethan life. She was also a lecturer for the Royal Academy of Dramatic Art and a member of the British Drama League, so she knew whatever there was to be known about dramatic writing. Dorothy, however, was diffident about her powers in this direction, in spite of the fact that most of the action in the Wimsey books is contained in pages of dialogue. With continual encouragement from Miss Byrne she "made a stab at it." She would write a few pages and send them over to St. John's Wood where Miss Byrne lived. Miss Byrne would then put the material in order, cut out the masses of extraneous business, and return it to Dorothy with notes as to how to proceed for the *theater.* Eventually the play, *Busman's Honeymoon,* was finished, and it opened in Birmingham in 1936, with Dennis Arundell playing Peter Wimsey. Miss Sayers thought he was perfect and tried to see that he was engaged whenever a dramatization of Wimsey was mooted. This was odd, because the general consensus of opinion at the time was that although Mr. Arundell was a splendid classical actor he was

WIMSEY NEARS HIS END

not particularly well cast as Wimsey. The play was, however, a great success and enjoyed a good London run. But Dorothy could not leave it there; she had to make use of all those splendid pages Miss Byrne had surgically removed from the drama, so she made the play into the final, *final* Wimsey book, also called *Busman's Honeymoon.*

This is, of course, the opposite way from the usual process. In the dedication to Muriel St. Clare Byrne, Helen Simpson and Marjorie Barber, Dorothy says of the book, which she calls "a love story with detective interruptions":

It has been said, by myself and others, that a love-interest is only an intrusion upon a detective story. But to the characters involved, the detective-interest might well seem an irritating intrusion upon their love-story. This book deals with such a situation. It also provides some sort of answer to many kindly inquiries as to how Lord Peter and his Harriet solved their matrimonial problem. If there is but a ha'porth of detection to an intolerable deal of saccharine, let the occasion be the excuse.

It is what used to be called before the days of permissive writing, "hot stuff." The love scenes are pretty torrid, and some of them in *French.* Peter remembers that a previous lady friend, one who "had every opportunity of judging," had said:

"ce blond cadet de famille ducale anglaise . . . il tenait son lit en Grand Monarque et s'y démenait en Grand Turc." The Fates, it seemed, had determined to strip him of every vanity save one. Let them. He could fight this battle naked. He laughed suddenly.
"Enfin, du courage! Embrasse-moi, chérie. Je trouverai quandmême le moyen de te faire plaisir. Hein? tu veux? dis donc!"

"Je veux bien," replied Harriet, with great expectations which did not go unfulfilled.

Busman's Honeymoon again gives us the frustrated spinster, Aggie Twitterton—a figure not of fun, but of extreme pathos.

The book opens with letters between members of the Wimsey family and their friends describing the Wimsey-Vane wedding, which had taken place at St. Cross Church, Oxford, "in the old, coarse Prayer-book form, and the bride said 'Obey.' " Gold lamé was produced in the thirties by a new process which brought it within the price range, not of everybody, but of more people than hitherto, so of course Harriet was married in it, although as Helen, Duchess of Denver, said, "a plain costume would have been more suitable"; but the tastes in dress of most of Dorothy's female characters were somewhat outlandish. Harriet, who was definitely stated to be twenty-nine in *Strong Poison* (1930), and reverted to twenty-eight in *Have His Carcase* (1932), must have been either way nearly forty at the time of her marriage. Considering that she went on to have three children at two yearly intervals she must have been very tough indeed. We can all have fun tripping up authors who use the same characters in a series. Dorothy did it herself with Arthur Conan Doyle.

The Dowager Duchess deals with the matter of renting a London house for the newly married pair, and decides on No. 2 Audley Square, which is now (and probably was then) the University Women's Club. She sets about engaging eight servants to supplement Bunter and the housekeeper—an unlikely number, even in 1938, when you could still get a housemaid for under £1 a week.

Dorothy always brought into her stories some topical event or controversy, and in *Busman's Honeymoon* she mentions the New Prayer Book, which was exercising the minds of both laity and clergy. "Helen," writes the Dowager Duchess in her diary,

obligingly presented us with a copy of the new form of marriage service, with all the vulgar bits left out—which was asking for trouble. Peter . . . said he knew all about the "procreation of children," in theory though not in practice, but that the "increase of mankind" by any other method sounded too advanced for him, and that, if he ever did indulge in such dangerous amusements, he would, with his wife's permission, stick to the old-fashioned procedure. He also said that, as for the "gift of continence," he wouldn't have it as a gift. . . .

Because Muriel St. Clare Byrne had kept the story line taut and economical, as it had to be for a play, all that Dorothy could do for the book was to fill it out with love scenes and quotations. Not content with Peter and Harriet breaking out into literary passages of arms on the slightest pretext, she also created the local police superintendent as a maniac in the same field. When the mystery is solved, Wimsey drives Harriet to Duke's Denver while the honeymoon cottage is being modernized. He introduces Harriet to the family portraits: "Here is Gerald, with a horse, by Furse; and downstairs . . . you will find a picture of a horse, with Gerald, by Munnings." And Harriet meets a family ghost.

Except for the final page the book is a lighthearted romp, and Dorothy wrote no more of Wimsey in book form. She resurrected the family for *The Spectator* in November 1939, using *The Wimsey Papers*—letters between members of the family—to comment on the war and hand out hints and information, such as how to walk in the dark during the blackout. Helen the stiff-necked duchess has joined the Ministry of Instruction and Morale, though, as her mother-in-law says:

What *she* can possibly have to instruct any one about I don't know, but as the place is packed with everybody's wives and nephews and all the real jobs seem to have been handed over to other departments it's as good a spot as any to intern the nation's trouble makers.

An elementary school for boys from the East End is quartered in the west wing at Denver, and of course Peter, now the father of two sons, is on some mysterious mission somewhere. Under the cover of Miss Climpson's meanderings, the government is castigated for silly trivialities:

. . . like the *school-children.* I expect it was *necessary* to get them *out* without any books or pencils or anything to the *nearest* available place; but I do think the Government might have *helped* the subsequent arrangements rather more, and got the schools together and *organised* the distribution of equipment and things.

Wimsey airs the anti-socialist views of his creator, as do the
Dean of Shrewsbury College, and Colonel Marchbanks, writing
from the Bellona Club:

Thank God, I say, we're not saddled with Russia as an ally, which we
should have been if some of our bright intellectuals had had their way.
Remember those dashed Socialists last August? Bursting into tears all
over the place, and prophesying the end of this country if we didn't
throw our arms round Comrade Stalin's neck.

These *Papers* were written weekly during the "phony" war
period, and they are valuable to social historians for recalling
small matters which have now been forgotten. (Even big matters too, for who now, apart from war historians, remembers the
Russo-Finnish campaign?) In January 1940, both in and out of
Parliament, there was pressure on the B.B.C. to reply to "Lord
Haw-Haw," whose identity was then unknown. At that time it
was Baillie-Stewart, who had achieved fame as the "Officer in
the Tower," where he had been confined for spying. He was,
in fact, the last official prisoner there. The ninth installment of
the *Wimsey Papers* is made up of letters to the Ministry of
Instruction and Morale, both for and against the idea of setting
up an anti-propagandist. The suggestion had first been made in
the House of Commons by Harold Nicolson. Miss Climpson put
forward the idea that while "Lord Haw-Haw" was speaking the
B.B.C. should simultaneously feed in hecklers "to make the
effect of a speaker being heckled at a public meeting! The
listeners could JOIN IN with shouts and cheers, and a GOOD TIME
would be had by all. This would, I am sure greatly appeal to the
SPORTING INSTINCTS of our people!" No action was taken,
either by the M.I.M. or the B.B.C.

The series ends suddenly with the eleventh installment on
January 26, 1940. It was headed by a "cover-all" announce-
ment: "Miss Sayers' articles will in future appear not as a weekly
series, but at less regular intervals." This could mean that she

had fallen out with *The Spectator,* had too much work ahead, or had just lost interest. No more articles appeared and she wrote nothing else about Wimsey apart from one or two substandard short stories. Oddly enough, for France had not yet fallen nor seemed likely to, Wimsey's last letter to his wife is strangely prophetic:

You are a writer—there is something you must tell the people, but it is difficult to express. You must find the words.

Tell them, this is a battle of a new kind, and it is they who will have to fight it, and they must do it themselves and alone. They must not continually ask for leadership—they must lead themselves. This is a war against submission to leadership, and we might easily win it in the field and yet lose it in our own country. . . . They (the people) must not look to the State for guidance—they must learn to guide the State. . . . I can't very well tell you just how and why this conviction has been forced upon me, but I have never felt more certain of anything.

Nowadays some middle-aged critics are apt to decry the Wimsey books as being snobbish and riddled with racial prejudice. It cannot be overlooked that evidence can be found for this, but evidence can also be found to prove the contrary. The snobbishness does not lie in the fact that she made Wimsey a member of the upper classes. That was all part of modernizing the King Arthur legend and because she knew that everyone loves a lord. It is her attitude to her readers which is snobbish. The constant use of classical quotations and long passages in French without giving a translation seems to indicate a certain contempt—"What! you don't understand Latin, Greek or French? Too bad. You can either find out or leave my books to those who do." This takes her refusal to "write down" to the reader a bit too far.

It has been said, both in her defense and Chesterton's, that what appears now to be anti-Semitism was common thought at the time. What they were both supposed to be against was not Jews per se but the way Jews manipulated the money markets.

The Marconi scandal and other questionable financial matters
reverberated through the twenties, as the Great Megatherium
scandal reverberated through the Wimsey books. It was not
until after the Second World War, when people first realized
the ultimate horror to which anti-Semitism can lead, that people, generally Americans, began to complain about Dorothy's
anti-Jewish remarks. She is, I think, a little more guilty than
Chesterton, if only because she appealed to a wider public.
Only *The Unpleasantness at the Bellona Club* and *The Nine
Tailors* have no pejorative remarks about Jews, leaving aside
Whose Body? in which, although the victim is Jewish, there are
only the Dowager Duchess's comments of the Jews as a race:

. . . Of course we're all Jews nowadays, and they wouldn't have minded
so much if he'd pretended to be something else, like that Mr. Simons
we met at Mrs. Porchester's, who always tells everybody that he got
his nose in Italy at the Renaissance, and claims to be descended some-
how or other from La Bella Simonetta—so foolish, you know, dear—
as if anybody believed it; and I'm sure some Jews are very good people,
and personally I'd much rather they believed something, though of
course it must be very inconvenient, what with not working on Satur-
days and circumcising the poor little babies . . . and never being able
to have bacon for breakfast.

Jews are sometimes dragged in quite unnecessarily. In *Five
Red Herrings* a commercial traveler is part of the plot, but there
is no reason why he should be Jewish, or why we should be
treated to a page or more written in listhps. There is another
example of this in *Have His Carcase.*

It 'ud go vell, eh? Lord Peter Vimsey in the title-rôle? The nobility ain't
much cop these days, but Lord Peter is vell known. He does somethings. Nowadays, they all vant somebody as does somethings.

Can Miss Sayers have thought Jews were funny and objects
of ridicule? Her publisher, on whom she relied for her liveli-
hood, was a Jew, but Victor Gollancz does not appear to have
made any comment, and no replies were sent to the American

complainants. Dorothy is also insufferably rude about "niggers," servants and the working class, and she has a complex about the Soviet menace. Some of her utterances are very hard to stomach in the climate of opinion which now exists.

But of course, children then were still learning to count backward by chanting "Ten Little Nigger Boys"; all the same, one would expect someone of Dorothy's talents to be a little ahead of common thought, and she probably thought she was. "I have given up trying to forecast what anybody will think about anything," she had written in 1931, "and shall confine myself strictly in future to seeing that I never write a book which I know to be careless and meretricious." It *is* meretricious to be gratuitously offensive to anyone. She would not be able to justify why Hallelujah Dawson had to be a black man, nor why some of the other characters had to be Jews. She liked to fill out her stories with "characters," and the words she puts into their mouths do mirror the thoughts and opinions of their "types," so her defense might be: "I am not voicing my *own* ideas, this is how those kinds of people would regard Jews, Negroes or socialists." Perhaps, but as these books were far too long she did not have to *prove* that she was able to depict characters. It is really all part of her boundless energy and high spirits; she was the last of the *jolly* ladies, who seem to have been the Creator's one-off effort, born to one generation and never tried again.

Writing long novels was only part of Dorothy's life at this time. Until 1931 she continued to work at Benson's. Nor did she neglect her duties as a wife, and she frequently grumbled about being left servantless and obliged to do all her own cooking and cleaning. She was contributing short stories to magazines in England and America, producing articles on anything that took her fancy, broadcasting and writing sheaves of letters. In 1936, Mr. C. W. Scott-Giles, who is now Fitzalan Herald Extraordinary, wrote to her pointing out an error in *Clouds of Witness* where, in the recitation of the Duke of Denver's titles, he is called Viscount Saint-George, a courtesy title which must have been held by his son, who, if he was an undergraduate in *Gaudy Night*, would have been born in 1917. By return of post Dorothy replied, acknowledging the error and, like Dr. Johnson, pleading "sheer ignorance." This was the beginning of a correspondence which went on for years, Dorothy sometimes writing by every post. Between them they worked out a pedigree and history of the Wimseys going back to the crusades. It was the Cyprus cat, commonly known as tabby and brought back by the crusading Wimsey, which formed the "domestic cat couched as to spring proper" of the Wimsey arms. The "three mice courant, argent" were, they decided, added in George III's reign to commemorate a hopeless siege laid to the virtue of his queen, "the farmer's wife" of the nursery rhyme, by an extremely obtuse Wimsey. All kinds of other bits of imitation history were concocted by Dorothy and Helen Simpson—pseudo-Johnsonian utterances, various scandals about a misalliance between a Wimsey and a tradesman's daughter. Drawings were provided by Mr. Scott-Giles and his wife. It was all a bit of a giggle, even rather childish it seems from this distance, but harmless. Dorothy, with her usual dislike of wasting anything she had put down on paper, had the material privately printed and circulated among her friends at Christmas—a quite expensive venture, as they were mounted in mock nineteenth-century type.

Mr. Scott-Giles was only one of the recipients of her letters. In 1927 Dorothy joined the Society of Authors and brought many grievances to their notice. She complained bitterly about James Agate's "unfairness"—a mild word in the circumstances —to members of the Detection Club. If the great man did not happen to like the book he was reviewing he gave away the plot, and as he disliked anything and everything about women (always excepting Sarah Bernhardt) he gave away their plots on principle. Dorothy had written to Agate, and to the literary

The Wimsey coat of arms

editors of his papers, but had only received "rude replies." There was another blight in this field: "a frightful female on *The Spectator* who slaughtered mysteries wholesale, but she was driven out by a subscriber of my acquaintance, who knew the editor." Dorothy was a leading figure in the Detection Club, which operated from 31 Gerrard Street in London. Its members were at pains to point out that they had no connection whatever with the Crime Club, but the perverse public continued, and still do, to see no difference between books about crime and those about detection. Dorothy enlivened things considerably by introducing all sorts of nonsense with candles and skulls into the enrolling ceremony, and composed an oath for initiates to swear:

PRESIDENT: Do you promise that your Detectives shall well and truly detect the Crimes presented to them, using those Wits which it shall please you to bestow upon them and not placing reliance upon, nor making use of, Divine Revelation, Feminine Intuition, Mumbo-Jumbo, Jiggery-Pokery, Coincidence or the Act of God?
CANDIDATE: I do.

Dorothy thought it all great fun, and carried the others along with her by her sheer exuberance. A few found it embarrassing, and shuffled unwillingly around, longing to get at the drinks and food; but hardly anyone was able to say no to Dorothy. She brought many famous writers in other fields to speak at the club. P. G. Wodehouse remembers an exhilarating dinner as her guest, and many of her radio fees went to pay the expenses of the club. In 1949 she became president and remained in office until her death. One of her joys was that the robes originally made for G. K. Chesterton fitted her perfectly. As Chesterton was over six feet tall and two yards around, this gives some indication of the size of Dorothy. She adored dressing up and in one of the last meetings she attended she played Mrs. Hudson in the Sherlock Holmes skit.

She was a mass of contradictions. Her public manner was always formidable, but this camouflaged a deep shyness. She talked incessantly, mostly about her craft, and managed, while continually burbling, never to give away a single thing about herself. It was years, for instance, before people who considered themselves her closest friends knew where she lived, or that she was married.

No one was ever better served by a publisher than was Dorothy by Victor Gollancz. It is true that he knew he had a money spinner and that a good bit of the rock in the foundations of his firm was provided by the Wimsey books. Apart from a shared passion for music they had little else in common, and what Dorothy, with that Red bee in her bonnet, thought about the Left Book Club she kept to herself. Most publishers' files are full of authors' complaint about lack of money, but there is a refreshing absence of this sort of correspondence between Dorothy and Gollancz. Money was scarcely ever mentioned, though she did get annoyed sometimes about his advertising methods. For *The Nine Tailors* Gollancz thought up a very tricksy gimmick. "It is not true that 100,000 people bought Miss Sayers' latest book," he wrote for a press advertisement. The figures 100,000 were in heavy type and the *Daily Express* abstracted the number and ran a headline, "100,000 copies of *The Nine Tailors* sold." This was manifestly absurd, and Dorothy was furious with Gollancz, who, somewhat crestfallen, had to explain that what he was going to do was to follow this advertisement with another saying, "100,000 people did not buy *The Nine Tailors* but —— people did," and so on. A gentleman called Cranton, who said he was the only person of that name in the London Telephone Directory, objected to it being given to a criminal in *The Nine Tailors,* and suggested that his business had suffered in consequence. He got short shrift from Gollancz and quickly withdrew his objection. No one seems to have noticed that a character called Cranton was mentioned in *Have*

His Carcase two years earlier. Thinking up names for characters, particularly for an author like Dorothy who has dozens per
book, is always hazardous. The one sour note in this author/pub-
lisher relationship came about over that precious "L."

I don't know whether I am a particularly trying and tiresome author
—I hope not—but I do admit to one fad. I do like my name to appear
in advertisements in the same form on which it stands on the title-
page: "Dorothy L. Sayers", and I do most particularly object to "Dorothy Sayers". I feel sure that I have mentioned it before, and I thought
you had got it right. So that I really was annoyed to find it all wrong
again in today's *Observer.* It is no doubt true that "Dorothy Sayers" is
easier to display, and if I had thought about this in the beginning of
things I would have adopted "D. L. Sayers" and stuck to it—but I
didn't, and, seeing that "Dorothy L. Sayers" has proved manageable
in the past, I think it might be managed again. My feeling about this
is no doubt unreasonable, but the fact remains that "Dorothy Sayers"
has unpleasant associations for me and I do not like it. It is, if you like,
a Freudian complex associated with my school days, and possibly I
ought to get over it, but I can't. It produces in me a reaction of humilia-
tion and depression and *I don't like it.* I am tired of writing letters of
protest to Brewer and Collins and the B.B.C. and the newspapers—and
when Mr. Gollancz, in his largest and blackest type, goes back on me
it does seem hopeless. After all, that is the signature I have chosen—
may I not have it? Other authors seem to get what they want: I don't
see allusions to Ethel Dell, or George Shaw, or Freeman Crofts . . .
Mayn't I have my "L"? I wish you would take this request seriously.
                                                    Yours despairingly.

All the London publishers looked askance at the advent of
Allen Lane's sixpenny Penguin paperback books, but to Gollancz, fairly new in the field, they seemed a particular threat.
He was adamant about the Sayers books, which he was already
bringing out at rock-bottom prices, and refused all Lane's ap-
peals to be allowed to bring them out under his green-covered
crime section. In February 1936, Lane thought he detected a
weakening in Gollancz's attitude and wrote again, a most reasonable letter, pointing out that a deal would be to their mutual
advantage, only to receive:

My dear Lane,

No!

Yours,

V.G.

Penguin did eventually bring out the Wimsey books, but not until much later, and Victor Gollancz Ltd. still manages to sell them in hardback in large enough numbers to make regular reprinting a viable proposition.

During the war publishers' activities were severely hampered by paper rationing. As always happens, a few newcomers arose to corner batches of precious paper, and mushroom publishers sprang up, made a killing, then faded out, often leaving authors, agents and merchants in the lurch. The government had badly underestimated the public's urgent hunger for reading matter. Gollancz had to fight off the blandishments of one of the fly-by-nights who was offering fabulous terms for the Wimsey books. He had, he said, served Miss Sayers very well. He had given her a large share of his ration—in fact from 1939–43 he had published almost half a million copies of her works. He was having trouble with his other authors, some of whose agents were threatening withdrawal from his list. One can understand the feelings of an author who has written a well-received book only to have it refused reprinting because of paper rationing. The sight of the umpteenth issue of a Dorothy L. Sayers on the bookstalls must have given him a jaundiced eye. On the other hand, Gollancz, who was a businessman, knew what he could sell. Dorothy does not seem to have bothered about these wranglings, and was content to leave them to be sorted out by her agents. She had enough to bother about with the stupid demands of readers: "Do I think that Hitler has some place in the Divine Order of things?"

If Gollancz was worried when Dorothy gave up writing detective books, he did not show it. He brought out most of her religious books and her plays. *The Man Born to Be King*

A postcard signed by Miss Sayers, 1942

alone has run into nearly thirty editions. He probably always hoped that another Wimsey would arrive one day, and she was always promising him that "straight" novel. She edited several volumes of detective stories for him, and contributed to *Double Death*, a story in which six authors each provided a chapter. Apart from the long Wimsey books there were three volumes of short stories. They are good of their kind, but I think she found the formula restricting. Some of them are extremely nasty. There is one where the murderer turns his victim into an art deco settee after electro-plating the body. Another concerns the search for an old gentleman's stomach in the wilds of Scotland. In one, Wimsey cheats at cards, for the best possible reason of course; in another, he has a false account of his death published in the newspapers. This does not really accord with the oath of the Detection Club. In "The Cave of Ali Baba," published in book form in 1928 but no doubt written much earlier for a magazine, there is a door electronically controlled to open only to the vibrations of one particular voice—Wimsey's. Such a thing is possible nowadays, but in the twenties it could only have been postulated, if anywhere, in scientific journals, which shows the wide range of Dorothy's reading, or the breadth of her much debated imagination.

The stories about the commercial traveler for a wine merchant, Montague Egg, seem to me quite amusing trifles, nothing more. Monty Egg appears to owe his creation in some measure to Chesterton's Father Brown. Where the Father helps himself along with a prayer, Egg has recourse to a rhyme from *The Salesman's Handbook*.

Don't wait for unpleasant disclosures to burst. If the truth must be told see that *you* tell it first.

> Be clean and courteous; raise your hat,
> And wipe your boots upon the mat:

> Such proofs of gentlemanly feeling
> Are to the ladies most appealing.

And he had much more in like vein.

Some of Dorothy's other short stories do not concern either Wimsey or Montague Egg. One, "An Arrow O'er the House," about the efforts of an unsuccessful novelist to publicize his works, is extremely funny. There is a mock-Gothic effort called "Scrawns" and the very sinister "Cyprian Cat." When mentioning the actor Garrick Drury in *Gaudy Night* Miss Sayers seems to have forgotten that she had already killed him off in a nice little piece, "Blood Sacrifice." But as she says of another writer, "it's the sort of thing that could happen to any of us."

The Gollancz/Sayers partnership was, and still is to a certain extent, a profitable partnership. Yet a mystery remains—in 1967 Gollancz made a bulk sale of Wimsey books to the firm of Palmolive-Peet. I have been unable to trace this transaction further and am left boggling at the thought of Dorothy L. Sayers, M.A. (Oxon.) Hon.D.Litt. (Durham), being given away with a bar of soap!

9

❧

War—and Broadcasting

Then there was Miss Dorothy L. Sayers who turned from a
life of crime to join the Church of England,
Extract from a schoolboy's essay

Looking back over the whole range of the Wimsey books one
can see trends in them now which were certainly not apparent
to the reader at the time they were written, and may have been
only dimly realized by the author. Dorothy needed money, and
primarily that is why the books were written; but toward the
end they became more than ever like morality plays—good
against evil, the terrible retribution that evil exacts. She was an
upholder of the law, and the law demanded death for the murderer. It is evident that this aspect of her work troubled her
conscience, and she meets it head on in the last chapter of
Busman's Honeymoon. Even then she had to make the murderer full of hatred, unrepentant and uncaring—a person who
justly deserved his fate. There was little agitation for the ending
of capital punishment in the thirties, and if there had been,
Dorothy would almost certainly have been on the side of the
hangers, even though the logical part of her recognized that
hanging did no actual *good* but was merely society exacting its
revenge. Society can make mistakes, as she showed in *Strong*

Poison, where but for the fact that Wimsey just happened to be at the trial, Harriet Vane would probably have been found guilty at her re-trial, and in fact was only proved innocent by a series of happy chances. But Dorothy did believe that hanging was a deterrent.

Certainly I allow that, once a person has seriously contemplated the act of murder, the fear of capital punishment is unlikely to deter him. What it does do is to prevent the majority of people from ever getting to the point when they can seriously contemplate such an act. The inhibition is produced I think, partly by the atmosphere of peculiar horror associated with the gibbet; but its effectiveness also depends on whether detection and execution are likely to follow pretty *certainly* upon the crime. For example, in this country, because of the capital penalty for murder, it is rare for the professional burglar to go armed. He doesn't mind doing time; but he does not want to "swing" for anything he might do in the excitement of the moment. In the States, the armed burglar is more common; there the death penalty does not follow automatically on conviction for murder; and if it is imposed there is always a good chance of wriggling out of it or getting it commuted. If you are proposing to commit murder, I should advise you to do it on the other side of the Atlantic; but if you think that anyone may have a motive for doing away with you, you will, on the whole, be safer here!

(Letter to Mr. Herbert Byard, October 1, 1945)

It is doubtful that Dorothy would have changed her mind had she lived longer. What she could see ahead in 1938 was the coming war, and this appalled her. Wimsey, with his facetiousness, his dabbling in this and that, did not fit in, and the detection of crime for amusement, no matter how scholarly the sleuth, did not fit in either. Besides, she had found another passion—the theater. She never stood on the edge, but dived right into anything which caught her interest. She adored all the trappings of the stage, picked up the jargon, and worshiped anyone connected with it. Dorothy was not, however, blind to the follies of actors, their vanities, and the way they tried to snatch advantage to themselves from any circumstance, as witness the letter from "Alan Float" to the Ministry of Instruction and Morale in *The Wimsey Papers*, with regard to the Lord Haw-Haw controversy:

Since the identity of the German broadcaster known as "Haw-Haw" seems to be arousing some public interest, may I offer a suggestion? His accent seems to me to resemble very closely (particularly in the vowel sounds) that used by (a) an actor of insufficient breeding and experience when impersonating an English aristocrat or (b) (more subtly) an experienced actor of good social standing impersonating a man of inferior breeding aping the speech of the English aristocracy. It is, in fact, very like the accent I use myself in the character of the self-made "Stanton" in "Dangerous Corner", which I have played with marked success in the West-End and in the Provinces (photograph and press-cuttings enclosed, with stamped addressed envelope for return). If it is decided to broadcast a reply to this propaganda, would you consider me for the part? . . . I should add that I have had several broadcasting engagements and can be trusted to give a good performance from a script at first reading.

Anyone who thinks actors do *not* behave like this should be at the receiving end of a television authority's telephone line when a performer in a soap opera is rumored to be, in reality, on his deathbed.

In 1936 Dorothy was approached by the Friends of Canterbury Cathedral to write a play for their festival of 1937. She chose for a subject not one of the better-known bishops or martyrs but William of Sens, the architect who rebuilt the cathedral after the disastrous fire of 1174. It is written in blank verse, and is an exploration of the sin of pride—the pride of William, not for himself, but for his work; his raging zeal for the house of God, missing out God Himself. God cannot be glorified by any kind of sin, and so William falls, symbolically, through a faulty rope. The title comes from the 69th Psalm: "The zeal of Thy house has even eaten me." Dorothy was always fascinated by the good which may come from evil, and the evil which often follows on good. As William explains:

> . . . A year ago
> An idle mason let the chisel slip
> Spoiling the saint he carved. I chid him for it,
> Then took the tool and in that careless stroke
> Saw a new vision, and so wrought it out
> Into a hippogriff. But yet the mason
> Was not the less to blame. So works with us
> The cunning craftsman, God.

William boasts of his certainty of God:

> We are the master craftsman, God and I—
> We understand one another. None, as I can,
> Can creep under the ribs of God, and feel
> His heart beat through those Six Days of Creation.

Dorothy must have heard many self-rightous priests and Christians make similar claims, though not half as poetically.

> He knows that I am indispensable
> To His work here; and for the work's sake, He,
> Cherishing, as good masons do, His tools,
> Will keep me safe.

boasts William. But then God shows him He will not accept such arrogant certainty. The play is well argued, even if it does seem to make God somewhat petty-minded and guilty of the very sin He condemns in William. From the theatrical point of view it is extremely "actable"—the only jarring note is the dragging in of an unlikely love interest. It was first performed in the Chapter House, June 12–18, 1937. Most of the costumes and props were made by the Friends and the cast. Dorothy herself spent many days stitching feathers on angels' wings. These costumes, which always had to be hired if a license to produce was to be obtained, came to a sad end. After serving many an amateur production they were put into storage during the war. When brought out for their first peace-time airing they were found to be verminous, and were unceremoniously destroyed on the roof of the building by the London County Council Pest Officer. Dorothy had loved them—so many of her hours had gone joyfully into their making—but her only comment on hearing the news was a shrug and an "Oh, well." She accepted something when it was really inevitable.

Harcourt Williams played William in *The Zeal of Thy House*, and shared the production with Frank Napier. These two, to whom Dorothy was intensely loyal, were bequeathed the rights of the play in her will. In 1938 it was given an entirely professional cast and moved to the Westminster Theatre, with Harcourt Williams, Frank Napier, and Michael Gough playing their original parts. It was seen there by Queen Mary, who is reputed to have made the comment, "What a *dear* little theatre this is! I never knew it was here, and I lived only just round the corner for years." The play subsequently moved to the Duke of York's and finally to the Garrick. In the cast was a young boy, Peter Graham Scott, now a well-known television producer, and he remembers, "Miss Sayers used to wander round the rehearsals like an amiable female Mao, gently correcting Harcourt Williams, who was rather an old school 'ham.' " He remembers too her extreme kindness—everyone in the cast, a large one, had a first-night present, and at the close, each was personally thanked. *The Zeal of Thy House* is a splendid play in the genre of religious drama, and it is a pity that it is no longer very highly rated.

Dorothy's Canterbury play of 1939 was not so successful. Called *The Devil to Pay*, it is a version of the Faustus story. What she intended doing was to supply "some kind of human interpretation to a supernatural legend." It was too much "in the mind" for the average playgoer and had only a four weeks' run. Some of its lack of success was due to Dorothy's insistence on having Harcourt Williams as Faustus. He had been excellent in *Zeal* but was too old for Faustus, and although he had always been a splendid supporting actor, and a very good director, he had never really made it as a leading man. He *was* a bit of a ham, and Dorothy was aware of this, yet there is scarcely any play of hers, either on stage or radio, in which he did not have a part. They may have been united by the same religious thought, for Williams often put on sacred drama at his own expense, and gave concerts in churches. In the printed version of *The Devil to Pay* there is a dedicatory poem "To the interpreter—Harcourt Williams." It is a little bit turgid, especially as it is prefaced by one of her own quotations: "What I have done is yours; what I have to do is yours; being part in all I have, devoted yours." Harcourt Williams, who was himself devoted to his wife and family, probably found this public avowal of gratitude somewhat embarrassing.

Dorothy did not do another stage play until 1946, when she wrote *The Just Vengeance* for Lichfield Cathedral's 750th anniversary. It was directed by Frank Napier, with music composed by Antony Hopkins. It is obviously a play written for a special occasion and a special place, and it never really comes to life. But Queen Mary, who had her accommodation nearby, liked it.

It is right, I think, to consider here Dorothy's last play for the stage, *The Emperor Constantine,* written for the Festival of Britain celebrations at Colchester in 1951. As a play it was anything but successful; I think it has a great many of the faults of the Wimsey books: over-discursive, setting off at angles, hammering home points already made plain and ignoring obscure ones. It starts with the legend that Helena, the mother of Constantine and the discoverer of the True Cross at Jerusalem, was the daughter of King Coel—the "old King Cole" of the nursery rhyme. The king and "his fiddlers three" spend most of the play asleep while the fortunes of Constantine are followed through twenty-six episodes by over a hundred people. The core of the play is the hammering out of the wording of the creed at Nicea in A.D. 325 by the bishops of the early church. The essence of the argument is contained in a few lines of Bishop Athanasius:

God is a spirit, and that which derives from Him is spirit also, begotten of Him as the ray is begotten of the light. The ray derives from the light, not subsequently, but simultaneously; and as there is no ray without light, so there is no light without the ray. Neither is the ray inferior to the light, for it is light—light out of light, from the very substance and being of light, as the Son is God out of God, from the very substance and being of God; therefore the blessed Apostle in his Epistle to the Hebrews, calls Him: "the brightness of the Father's glory and the express image of His person, upholding all things by the word of His power". And the Apostle John, in the beginning of his Gospel which lies here open before you, declares very well both the distinct Person of the Son and His equal Godhead with the Father, saying: "In the beginning was the Word, and the Word was *with* God, and the Word *was* God".

The scene goes on—and on. The good people of Colchester, who thought they were going to see Old King Cole exposed by Lord Peter Wimsey, drifted away in polite puzzlement. Although Miss Sayers admirably expounded her *own* theology, it was not that of the Church of England as understood by the bulk of her followers. They could understand a Trinity of Father, Son and Holy Ghost; Christ as the *Son* of God and the Holy Spirit emanating from them both; but that they were all One was too difficult for the general laity to follow, especially as the majority of a theater audience would probably be non-religious; and of course, this doctrine is not that of all Christians. Rehearsals had been difficult, punctuated by clashes with the festival director. Costumes were designed by Norah Lambourne and made by members of the Colchester Women's Institutes. Dorothy helped to make the jewelry and was always proud of her efforts in this line. A great deal of help was given, from the army

who provided soldiers to the School of Art whose students
helped with the scenery; but it was not a happy experience. On
the first night the play ran for nearly four hours, at the end of
which Dorothy took a curtain call in a white linen costume,
badly creased and dipping up and down round the hem, white
stockings and tennis shoes. She loomed over the footlights like
Lot's wife in her transformation. The work, however, should
not be belittled. It contains the root and branch of Dorothy's
personal faith, and is argued with high intelligence. It just did
not make a good theatrical experience.

During the years Dorothy had been writing books and plays
for the stage, she had also been active in broadcasting. She had
contributed to the omnibus detective serial "Behind the
Screen," in May and June 1930, and had taken part in a discussion, "Plotting a Detective Story," with Anthony Berkeley in
July of the same year. In December the B.B.C. asked her to
approach Agatha Christie, Anthony Berkeley, E. C. Bentley,
Freeman Wills Crofts and Clemence Dane to write another
serial. She was empowered to offer each writer fifty guineas,
while her own fee as coordinator was to be seventy-five guineas.
These were enormous fees for the time, and indeed not far
below today's rates for similar work; but this was the only way
the still young corporation could persuade well-known per-
sonalities to work for it, as many of the better-known writers,
and actors too, were somewhat contemptuous of this new
medium. "The Scoop," as the serial was called, seems to have
started on the air before the final scripts were completed. Dorothy flung herself into the project with typical enthusiasm. "I
love the mike," she caroled, and could not understand why
"Christie seemed bored." She apologized for her bad typing, to
which the B.B.C. avuncularly replied, "It is part of *our* job to
do the typing." (Shades of more gracious days!)

The serial was well received but there were twenty-five objections to Dorothy's bad language in the final episode. "I can

see nothing objectionable about God," was her tart reply; any-way, it was the job of the B.B.C. censor to cut out the swearing. She found all the contributors friendly, only Miss Christie was a bit awkward because "she disappears and won't argue." These two ladies both suffered from shyness—in Dorothy it took the form of extroversion, in Agatha Christie just the opposite. Any-one who has worked with her is well acquainted with her habit of withdrawing from anything that threatens to be a "scene." She sees the signals way ahead of anyone else, and when the argument arrives she is just not there. No one loved an argu-ment more than Dorothy, and it is surprising she found Christie merely "awkward."

Dorothy seems to have been a most willing broadcaster throughout 1931–4 on almost any subject. There was even a suggestion that Mac should give a talk on cookery, but I cannot trace that it was ever delivered. Dorothy helped to launch "Consider Your Verdict," a program which was first mooted in July 1932 and has, in various forms, been running ever since. There was a row in 1931, with internal rockets flying hither and thither, about the omission of that "L." from her name; even the distinguished chief announcer did not escape. Then in 1934 came an irate postcard: "Please take steps to see that my name is removed from any further programme announcements, as the Director of Talks is unable to give it correctly." Apart from giving permission for broadcasts of several of her short stories, she turned down all B.B.C. offers for the next four years.

In May 1938 it was suggested she should be asked to write a nativity play, no doubt because of the success of *Zeal of Thy House*. By this time she was not the most popular lady among the B.B.C. hierarchy. It was said she was difficult about money; and she always wanted to do her own casting and had ideas about production. Permission was grudgingly given for the offer to be made, provided she understood that she had no say in the casting. She could attend rehearsals, but could not attempt to produce. This rather jaundiced view of Dorothy is not borne out by Val Gielgud, who produced the nativity play. She never interfered, he says; she would make notes, always to the point, and hand them to him to deal with as he thought fit. She did, however, suggest Harcourt Williams and Raf de la Torre for parts, and got them. The nativity play, *He That Should Come*, was a great success, and among the people who wrote letters of appreciation was Mrs. Winston Churchill.

Once back in broadcasting Dorothy seems never to have stopped. She contributed to a series of talks, "Christ of the Creeds." Following a discussion by Bishop Talbot she finds "it hasn't occurred to him to mention Sin!!! You wouldn't think anyone *could* overlook that theological trifle would you? Consequently I have had to squash Sin into two minutes filched from the Incarnation." She did talks for the Empire Service, "Woman's Hour" and the armed forces' programs. Dorothy also appeared on "Any Questions," after which a luncheon bill for six shillings, sixpence—part of her reclaimable expenses—was bandied from the producer to the Accounts Department and back as being "rather excessive," until some more exalted set of initials scrawled "Pay it" across the memo, and brought the bill to rest in the appropriate file. In 1940 the government considered enlisting the B.B.C.'s help with an anti-gossip campaign. An outline Ministry of Information leaflet was sent to Dorothy with a request that she should contribute. It is quite possible that she was working for the government in an advertising capacity—some of the Ministry of Food rhymes have a strong flavor of Monty Egg's *Salesman's Handbook*. She was disturbed by the proposed format of the anti-gossip leaflet, thinking it was rude and contemptuous, and objected particularly to the term "Jay-talker." "The campaign," she wrote, "is too sneering, too negative, too meanly expressed," and she gave one or two suggestions for slogans:

Hitler dare not let his people talk. We know the British people *will* not talk. Your King and Country trust you.

and

You have seen a well-trained dog carrying a basket full of eggs. They are safe as long as he keeps his mouth shut. You carry the secrets of Empire and lives of a million men. Hold fast!

The Ministry of Information dropped the scheme, which was just as well considering the outcry there was about posters telling how to use handkerchiefs. By 1940, the Religion Department of the B.B.C., as the telephone operator at Broadcasting House informed callers, had "all gone to Bristol"—an extremely unwise move as it was to turn out, and a place to which Dorothy refused to travel; the consequence was a high expenditure in telegrams. Replying to a query from the Reverend Eric Fenn about a press release, Dorothy said:

Suggest omit regular churchgoing deeply depressive average publican and sinner why describe me at all either they know me or they don't Dorothy L. Sayers please not Dorothy Sayers.

Quite a lot of things about the B.B.C.'s religious broadcasting annoyed her:

I always thought it unfair to put "Lift Up Your Hearts" just before the 8 o'clock News so that one can't escape it—like the vicar waylaying the congregation at the church door. But now Derek McCulloch has started it on the 6 o'clock I am foaming at the mouth, and the blasphemy in my household would shock Satan himself. I *won't* be prayed at and over and round like this! It's slimy, that's what it is, simply slimy. I think I shall apostasize and become a Zoroastrian or a Buddhist, or something that doesn't take a mean advantage of a person.

On July 17, 1941, her fury was boundless:

I spent Tuesday night up to one in the morning writing a solemn protest against that atrocious broadcast about P. G. Wodehouse. Did you ever hear anything more indecent? No doubt something had to be said about him, but why they should have chosen the most notorious contributor of the most notorious trash paper to deliver a talk, so vulgar and so envenomed by spite, passes my comprehension. We were all flabberghasted. (I like my secretary's improved spelling, will not alter it.) One usually accuses the B.B.C. of too much public school gentility but this comes straight out of the gutter. As for the nauseating scriptural parallel, it turned my stomach. I hope that some of you people in the Religious Department have had something to say about it.

P. G. Wodehouse, who was even then near sixty, had been caught by the sudden overwhelming of France by the Germans. He was interned at first under extremely bad conditions, but recommendations were made on his behalf by the Americans. They pointed out that if this elderly, and at the time, sick man, who was moreover a world-famous author, should die in prison, it would prove to the world what heartless vandals the Germans were. Wodehouse was released to house arrest; and perhaps a little foolishly, but no doubt in gratitude to the Americans, he consented to give some talks on the radio for transmission in the U.S.A. America was not then a belligerent, and the talks contained nothing but descriptions of the way France was coping. The splenetic talk branding Wodehouse as a traitor was broadcast by "Cassandra" of the *Daily Mirror.* Why the B.B.C. allowed it to go on has been argued over ever since, and practically everybody has apologized to Wodehouse, who on release went straight to America and stayed there. Although Williams of the Religious Department assured Dorothy that "the floor had been pretty thoroughly wiped by the culprit," hers was one of the very few voices raised on Wodehouse's behalf at the time. It did not do *her* much good, though. Her next talk in the "Postscript" series was canceled. The reason given was that

. . . it was not up to our Sunday standard. It preaches. It digs at mothers, doctors, agriculturalists and capitalists, rather in the manner of a Somerville debating society. Mr. Gates and Sir Walter Monckton agree. We suggest the lady be turned down on programme grounds. I don't know her. Can those who do say whether she would be likely to be persuaded to lay off religion and tackle, e.g. the problem of how war and peace are affecting and will affect the status of women.

The talk, "Living to Work," is published in a book of essays called *Unpopular Opinions* and there is nothing in it to warrant the spitefulness of the above memo. It was left to poor George Barnes, the director of the talks, to explain why the talk was rejected and to waffle on about the public being so stupid as not to like women's voices—a long-held tenet among the *men* in broadcasting, and useful as a means of keeping as many women as possible from the microphone and from promotion within the corporation. Dorothy accepted all this with her usual phlegmatism and Barnes sought to mollify her a few days later with the news that Lady Cripps was anxious to meet her.

Dorothy L. Sayers was, however, a force with which the B.B.C. had to reckon. The nativity play *He That Should Come* was extremely successful, and in March 1940 the Reverend J. W. Welch, the director of Religious Broadcasting, wrote to her suggesting that she should do a series of programs for the Children's Hour Department on the life of Christ. Replying that she would be willing to consider such a project, she stipulated that she must be permitted to introduce the person of Christ, and that the plays would be written in the modern idiom. At least this is what she is supposed to have laid down, for there is no letter on the files actually containing these conditions. Perhaps she made these points verbally, or may even have thought them up to exonerate the B.B.C. when a storm broke later. It is difficult to see the reason for any such conditions. *He That Should Come* was written in modern English, and it is not possible to write a twelve-part serial of a life *without* bringing in the subject. Besides, L. du Garde Peach had been writing Bible plays for Children's Hour for years in fairly modern speech. From this distance he seems to have had a tendency to write down to children, but forty years ago children were not so sophisticated as they are now.

Dorothy's conditions were accepted after Ogilvie, B.B.C.'s Director General, had consulted the Lord Chamberlain about the personification of Christ. Actually there was no need for this as radio plays were not subject to the Lord Chamberlain's scrutiny, but Ogilvie wanted to be on the safe side. The Lord Chamberlain could see no objection to the plays, but added it would be a quite different matter if ever it were proposed to televise them. With characteristic speed Dorothy set to work. From the first she wanted Val Gielgud as producer but was told that this was not possible; the cycle was to be done by Children's Hour, not by the Drama Department, and as Children's Hour was now in Bristol with Religion, it was much better for Derek McCulloch to have overall charge. She accepted the news with resignation and wrote to McCulloch saying how much she was looking forward to working with him, but in July she added a postscript to a long letter to Dr. Welch:

I am still obstinately set upon Val Gielgud's production. Very likely it is impossible. I do not care if it is. If the cursing of the barren fig tree means anything, it means that one must do the impossible or perish, so it is useless to tell me that it is not the time for figs.

It seems an odd reading of this particular Bible story! The letter is worth quoting more fully, as it sets out her ideas about the project.

What I have been considering with regard to the Children's Hour plays on the life of Christ is the general theme of the whole series. The thing must have a direction and unity as a complete work, apart from the unity of each separate play, so that it can build into a reasoned structure theologically as well as historically.

The theme I want to take is particularly that of the Kingship of Christ. At this moment, even children can't help knowing that there is a great dispute going on about how the world should be governed, and to what end, and I think they are fully capable of understanding what the meaning of the quarrel is, if the situation and arguments are put before them in a simple and vivid way. I shall make this business of the Kingdom the framework of the series, and choose incidents that will bring out this aspect of the story. . . .

The first play will probably be the most difficult to get going on, because it has to set the key for the rest, as regards style, language, treatment etc. I am trying to get to work on this now. . . .

It looks as though I should have to pull myself together and really make up my mind about Judas;—what *did* the man imagine he was doing? Pilate and Caiaphas and the rest are quite understandable, and from their own point of view highly respectable—one sees exactly what they were after—but Judas is an insoluble riddle. He can't have been awful from the start, or Christ would never have called him. I mean, one can't suppose that He deliberately chose a traitor in order to get Himself betrayed—that savours too much of the *agent provocateur,* and isn't the kind of thing one would expect of any decent man, let alone of any decent God—to do. And He can't have been so stupid as to have been taken in by an obviously bad hat;—quite apart from any doctrinal assumptions. He was far too good a psychologist. Judas must have been a case of *corruptio optima pessima;* but what corrupted him? Disappointment at finding that the earthly kingdom wasn't coming along? or defeatism, feeling that the war was lost, and one had better make terms quickly? Or just (as the Gospels seem rather unconvincingly to suggest) money and alarm for his own interests? If we can get a coherent Judas we can probably get a coherent plot.

Most of the plays were in outline by October and Dorothy and McCulloch were discussing casting. Frank Napier was working on munitions, and Raf de la Torre, at thirty-five, would probably be called up to serve in the military. These were the first two favorites for Christ. "We shall probably," as Dorothy said,

have to look for someone older, or with a physical disability, since we don't want to have to change Christs in the middle of the stream. It is a difficult part to cast, because we want, not only intelligence, biddableness, and a sympathetic feeling for what the thing is all about, but also a voice that is both flexible and of unmistakeable quality. It is important, especially as we can't *see* Christ, that when he speaks we should immediately get the feeling: *Ecce Homo.* (Unhappily, most actors who possess that kind of voice are only too horribly aware of the fact.)

McCulloch suggested Michael Redgrave or Robert Donat. Robert Donat would do, agreed Dorothy; "the one kind of Christ I absolutely refuse to have at any price is a *dull* Christ." Did Dr. Welch know the Chief Rabbi? If so, would he ask him to supply a suitable hymn for the Last Supper scene? The Chief Rabbi, Dr. Herz, obliged by return of post with the words of "Adon Olam," which he thought would meet the case.

It was decided to extend the plays, which had now been given the series title *The Man Born to Be King*, from thirty to forty-five minutes, which had both its advantages and drawbacks. As Dorothy wrote to McCulloch, "the thing, suddenly released from compression within thirty minutes, shot out like a joyful jack-in-the-box, and had to be captured and brought back." She had been sent one of L. du Garde Peach's plays on St. Paul as a timing guide, and wrote,

It's still about a page and a half longer . . . but there are not so many shipwrecks and effects to allow for. But I took the opportunity of the extra fifteen minutes to enliven things with a bit of crowdage and shoutery by introducing the famous episode of the Golden Eagle. This seemed good to me, as counteracting the necessarily rather pious and domestic effect of the Bethlehem scene. (I hate coping with this baby stuff—thank Heaven, one can only be young once, whoever one is!) It also gives Herod a good kick-off for his fury in the matter of the Massacre of the Innocents. It's important that this shouldn't be looked on as a mere piece of meaningless savagery. It was a perfectly reasonable political step, if you once allow that the good of the state is more important than the rights of the individual. The thing one wants to put up against the *idea* of the Kingdom of Heaven is the *idea* of the political kingdom, not the caprice of one wicked man. And finally, it gives Herod a final flare-up in his best manner—he handled that business rather well—and, as you will perceive, I have a weakness for the brilliant old ruffian. To the actor, of course, he is money for jam. I don't think anyone could go wrong in playing Herod, though I do rather see Cecil Trouncer in it, if he's available.

He was available, and did, in fact, play the part in the first production of the plays. Dorothy then proceeded with a long lecture on the production of radio plays. How the very busy and highly experienced Derek McCulloch took it can only be guessed at. The letter runs for six closely-typed quarto pages, and even to sit and read it must have taken a sizable chunk out of the working day; but he did have the advantage of being in Bristol, too far off except for telephone calls of the highest priority.

"In the hope," concludes Dorothy,

that you may find the play workable I will proceed with the next. I'm alarmed by the sweat this one has taken. . . . I hope you like the general title of the plays. It is an old fairy-tale title and tells the story in six words.

In December, as she wrote to Dr. Welch, she was still struggling with John the Baptist, and cursing the difficulty of getting any effect on the radio out of a scene with a lot of people in it.

It's such a nuisance not to be able to introduce, say, an elderly Pharisee suddenly, without having someone *say*, (in effect) "this voice that you are going to hear is that of a Pharisee and he is elderly"; and to remember that if more than three people take part in a conversation at once, the audience will get them hopelessly mixed up. That's the trouble I always suffer from when listening to a Radio play—especially if all the voices are of the same sex. As we get on into the Ministry, the overwhelming maleness of everybody is going to be a great trial. One can't help wishing that Christ's female acquaintances had been a little more varied and respectable. One can't do much, for children, with the Woman taken in Adultery or the lady who had had seven husbands, of whom the latest, and probably all the others, was of very dubious status, or with Mary Magdalen—except by giving a general impression that she lived a fast life and probably had too many cocktails. Who, I wonder, was Salome, who suddenly turned up at the graveside? I'm going to make her an old friend of John the Baptist's people, and so get her placed at the start. And I'm making Judas turn up early too. He lived at Kerioth and was a follower of John; but when he saw that Jesus was, so to speak, the coming man, he hitched his wagon to that star. His idea was to bring in the Kingdom socially and politically, and he saw in Jesus the sort of "inspired idiot" who could be at once a leader and a tool—rather like Hitler to the Ribbentrops and Goerings. (I don't mean that Judas intended anything as sinister as the Ribbentrops, but that he envisaged that kind of relationship.) He falls, in fact, to the very temptation that Christ resists in the wilderness—that of using the kingdoms of the world to bring in the Kingdom of God. Therefore he will have much the most practical turn of mind of all the disciples, and that is why they put him in charge of "the bag". So far, so good—and Christ accepts him, because there must always be some contact between the Kingdom and the world, and there must be, in a church, somebody with practical ability. But with that sort of person there is always "from the beginning" the danger of corruption—which duly occurs. That seems to fit in all right, and has the proper sort of tragic inevitability. But how all this is going to be got over to the youthful mind I don't know. There's nothing very simple about the "simple Gospel" when you look into it. It's about adult people and it's all very complex.

Golly, this is a job. Look at all those twelve disciples—and we know *nothing* about most of them. John has a personality, and Peter, and Judas, and Thomas Didymus; James, Philip, and Andrew have about two lines apiece, which throw no light on their characters; and they *all* have to be assembled and talk plausibly in the Upper Room. The Gospel *must* be a narrative of fact; nobody *inventing* a story could be so vague and slipshod about the *dramatis personae!*

In spite of worries about the drama of the project, most of which she worked out in letters such as the above, all seemed to be going well until January 1941, when McCulloch's lady assistant rashly returned the script of the first play with suggested alterations. Had this letter come from McCulloch himself, Dorothy would no doubt have grumbled and fought for her points, but would have carried on. After all, she was a good hand at telling *other* people how to do their jobs. Coming from a "glorified secretary" it was insupportable! She returned her contract to the B.B.C. torn into hundreds of small pieces. Confronted by this envelope full of confetti the corporation had two choices: to drop the project altogether, or to give in to Dorothy's insistence that the producer should be Val Gielgud or no one. It was, internally, a very difficult matter. McCulloch was the senior producer on Children's Hour, Gielgud was the rising man in Drama—two completely different departments. McCulloch felt aggrieved, Gielgud extremely embarrassed. What he did not need at that moment was the loud trumpeting on his behalf from this *enfant terrible*, and he definitely did *not* want to go to Bristol. A compromise was reached whereby the series was transferred to the Drama Department, with Gielgud as producer, to be bought back, as it were, by Children's Hour. All that Dorothy cared about was that she had got her own way and the producer of her choice, but the arrangement led to interdepartmental squabbles later on in the year as to who should pay the production costs. If it was all to be borne by Children's Hour, their budget would allow for only one play to be broadcast monthly. The original idea had been to put them out twice monthly to cover the period from Christmas to Easter. Were they, Children's Hour asked with some asperity, to cut out all their other items? For this is what would have to happen if their department were to bear the full cost. Arrangements were made for a special allocation for the series. Discussions were still going on about casting. The original idea was to have the whole cast possibly—but Christ definitely—played anonymously. This idea was dropped because of the difficulty of getting actors to agree to be heard without credits, and because many of them had instantly recognizable voices which would defeat the whole exercise and might lead to a kind of witch hunt by the press. The choice for Christ eventually settled on Robert Speaight. He was chosen because he was "known to be a devout Christian" and because of his great success as Becket in T. S. Eliot's *Murder in the Cathedral.*

By December 1941, five of the plays in the cycle were completed, and the first was scheduled for broadcasting over Christmas. On the tenth of the month Welch asked Dorothy if she would attend a press conference. This was an error of judgment on his part. Dorothy did not like the press, and had often been

A rehearsal of *A Man Born to Be King*, 1942. Miss Sayers with Robert
Speaight (center) and Val Gielgud

extremely rude to them. Throughout the Wimsey books newspapers and reporters are depicted in an unfavorable light. Because she was shy of making statements in public, she became
truculent, and treated the reporters somewhat contemptu-
ously, at the same time trying to impress upon them the great
novelty of what she was doing. Somewhat puzzled, because
after all, the Scriptures in contemporary language were not all
that novel, one of the reporters asked for a specimen of her
dialogue, and she obliged with a couple of extracts. It was a P.R.
exercise which did not come off in the manner intended, and
was quite unnecessary. The plays would have stood on their
merit without any pre-publicity. As it happened, the reporters,
having the benefit of a lull in hard news, took their revenge on
this "snooty female." The whole thing was sensationalized
beyond belief. "Life of Christ in slang" yelled the *Daily Mail,*
and went on to vilify Dorothy to such an extent that she threatened a libel action. Anti-B.B.C. hysteria was whipped up by the
Lord's Day Observance Society, who took a whole page of advertising in *The Church of England* newspaper, to set forth its
protest.

12th December, 1941

The Council of the Lord's Day Observance Society, at its meeting
today, had under consideration the Press announcements of a radio
innovation on a Sunday afternoon in the New Year of a Play entitled
"The Man Who Was Born to Be a King" [*sic*], in which the voice of our
Blessed Lord is to be introduced by a Shakespearian actor.

My Council desire to inform the B.B.C. that this proposed theatrical
exhibition will cause much pain to devout Christian people, who feel
deeply that to impersonate the Divine Son of God in this way is an act
of irreverence bordering on the blasphemous. It is a contemplated
violation of the Third Commandment which forbids taking the name
of God in vain.

The B.B.C., by its recent continentalising of Sunday Broadcasts with
Music Hall and Jazz programmes, has already distressed multitudes of
good citizens. We therefore make an earnest appeal to the B.B.C.

Authorities to respect what remains of the hallowed hours of the Lord's Day, and to refrain from staging on the wireless this revolting imitation of the voice of our Divine Saviour and Redeemer.

Fellow readers were asked to "write in your thousands" to ask the B.B.C. to "ban this Christ-Dishonouring Proposal."

The editor of the paper wrote to Dr. Welch that, for his part, he thought the "Christian influence of these plays on vast multitudes who are outside the church will be great," and added:

You will notice that Mr Martin of the Lord's Day Observance Society has broken out, but I cannot help feeling that all this is to the good, because it attracts attention to the broadcasts.

It certainly did draw attention to the broadcasts. Hundreds of letters reached the B.B.C. complaining about blasphemy. In the House of Commons, on December 19, the following question was asked:

SIR PERCY HURD (Unionist M.P. for Devizes): What steps does
    the Minister propose to take to stop this offence?
MR. THURTLE (Minister of Information): None.

So it must have seemed to Mr. Martin that even the government was on the side of Darkness, and he set aside £1200 to fight the B.B.C.—and gained for the corporation untold thousands in publicity, all this before a single line of any of the plays had been broadcast. In spite of his laconic answer in the House of Commons, the Minister of Information informed the Director General that the government did not want the country to be riven with religious controversy at that moment, so a meeting of the Central Religious Advisory Committee was called. Unfortunately it was not possible to get them all together at short notice, but copies of the script of the first play were sent to them. Thirteen out of fourteen members were in favor of going ahead, but some of the governors of the B.B.C. still dithered. On December 20, 1941, Welch sent them an impassioned memo:

None of us expected the two paragraphs in the cheaper press would have caused so much trouble. Undoubtedly it has prejudiced some people against the plays who would otherwise have been convinced of their moving sincerity. I have worked for two years on these plays as theological editor, and Miss Sayers has made them her *magnum opus,* and has written, if I may say so, herself and her religion into them. She is an artist, and has been working not only under the influence of her creative genius, but under a compelling sense of making an important religious contribution to our age. I need not add that her Christology is advanced and her treatment most reverent. She believes passionately in the integrity of her work, and is not likely to accept blue-pencilling to satisfy all the critics. Either she is right or she is wrong in what she is doing, and I, as Director of Religious Broadcasting stand or fall by her. . . . I have no shadow of doubt that the plays will be a moving and religious experience for possibly millions of listeners, outside or loosely attached to the church. I believe absolutely in what we are trying to do, and my four colleagues have pledged me their fullest support in what they also believe to be right. . . . What we are hoping to do through these plays is precisely what the medium of the microphone should do for Christian religion and the Church of God. I am glad to add that the Director General is also wholeheartedly of this opinion.

The Bishop of Winchester, who was chairman of the C.R.A.C., also approved.

The plays went ahead to diminishing protests from the antis—

No actor without blasphemy can represent the voice of Christ. "He spake as never man spake." The B.B.C. is not capable of reversing that truth. To place imaginary words on His lips is perilously near sacrilege.

—and rising approbation from the pros:

I am sure I am voicing the opinion of hundreds of my fellow clergy and thousands of my fellow Christians when I urge that the Director of the B.B.C. should turn a deaf ear to this undignified agitation.

Many people were angry at the attempts by the Lord's Day Observance Society to censor their listening, and pointed out that the views of this society were those of a *minority* of professing Christians, who were in any case a minority in the nation. It was pointed out that the voice of God had been heard for hundreds of years in the old morality plays and Christ was personalized every ten years at Oberammergau.

Eventually the voice of common sense prevailed.

It seems strange that objection should be taken to the words of our Lord being recited on the radio by an actor, when no objection is taken to His words being daily recited by countless clergy, schoolmasters and others with no particular qualifications to render them.

No objections were taken either to the rendering of portraits of Christ in paintings and sculptures, or to the fact that the Scriptures were often read by actors in broadcast services because they were better at it than the clergy.

Protests surged up again when the series was repeated in 1943. The *Glasgow Herald* ran an advertisement from the General Association of the Free Church of Scotland complaining of the "vast irreverence in the conception" and announcing a petition to the King containing thirty thousand signatures. Before this happened Gollancz had brought out the plays in book form, with full cast lists and Dorothy's notes to the producer on the various characters. Welch wrote an introduction, outlining the story of the commissioning of the series, and an account of the protest. Dorothy also supplied a preface in which she wrote:

My object was *to tell that story* to the best of my ability, within the medium at my disposal—in short, to make as good a work of art as I could. For a work of art that is not good and true *in art* is not good or true in any other respect, and is useless for any purpose whatsoever—even for edification—because it is a lie, and the devil is father of all such.

She paid generous tributes to the actors, the producer, and the B.B.C. and added, with a wickedness she could not resist:

It is moreover irresistibly tempting (though is it kind or Christian?) to mention the Lord's Day Observance Society and the Protestant Truth Society, who so obligingly did all our publicity for us at, I fear, considerable expense to themselves. Without their efforts, the plays might have slipped by with comparatively little notice, being given at an hour inconvenient for grown-up listening. These doughty opponents secured for us a large increase in our adult audience and thus enabled the political and theological issues in the most important part of the story to be treated with more breadth and pungency than might otherwise have seemed justifiable. . . . The irony of the situation is, however, not of my making—it is part of the universal comedy. Let us record the plain fact: the opposition did us good service; let our gratitude for that go where all gratitude is due.

Apart from this Dorothy had little to say about the controversy. It seems to have amused her more than scarring her soul. She knew she had done a good job, which was the essential thing; people's opinions were not important. She congratulated Val Gielgud on his O.B.E. in January 1942, "Just fancy your being decorated by H.M. when you are living in the Temple of Blasphemy!"

Dorothy listened to the plays at home with Mac: "My husband said it was a 'good show' and added that we'd got a good Christ—he's not strong on religion." This "gruff warrior" listened to the second play with "tears in his eyes." The criticism of bad language in the Crucifixion scene she dismissed with "you can't expect crucified robbers to talk like Sunday School teachers—the children won't mind, they *like* blood and tortures."

Apparently a Jewish acquaintance of Robert Speaight had been greatly impressed by the plays, for Dorothy wrote to Speaight:

Many congratulations to us on having done our bit towards the con-
version of the Jews! I believe they are supposed to be the hardest
nuts to crack—unless, of course, they just slide into it for social
reasons, or because they wish to be mistaken for Gentiles, which
doesn't really count—so between us we must have sounded quite convincing.

She thought the second production for Holy Week, 1944,

stood up pretty well to being done a second time. Sometimes, when
the original excitement has worn off the fabric of a script seems to go
thin, like linen when the dressing has been laundered out, and then
it becomes only too obvious that the stuff won't wear. But I'm encouraged to hope that it may hold together for a few years anyhow, if they
don't make it threadbare by too much repetition.

For the time being it all ended with thanks from B. E. Ni-
cholls, the Controller, and an offer of a set of twenty-five double-
sided records as a "souvenir." She accepted this somewhat
bulky memento with grace: "I am deeply grateful to the B.B.C.
for having entrusted me with this important and enthralling
piece of work." And she asked for an album of the actors' photographs. She had spent three years on the project, for an initial
fee of £50 per play. The B.B.C. had a pretty good bargain for
their £600.

There were repeats of the Passion sequences at Easter in
1944, '45 and '46, and in 1947 the whole series was redone with
Raf de la Torre as Christ and Noel Iliffe producing. She did not
think

the B.B.C. should grind them out every Holy Week till Kingdom come.
... I may be wrong but my own strong feeling is that the thing is being
badly overdone. The B.B.C. has spent a lot of money on them and
naturally wants to see a return, but this looking forward to a steady
annual hurdy-gurdy does appal me. The plays are a fairly good job of
work, but if they were a masterpiece of genius, they couldn't stand up
to that kind of thing without losing freshness.

Of the plays themselves, there is little new to be said. They
are of a uniform excellence, and they *were* a breakthrough in

religious broadcasting. They did bring Christ the Man and Christ the Son of God into the household, speaking a language all could understand, though the examples of "U.S. slang" are hard to find. The cycle was splendidly produced, and acted by a first-rate cast and at a time when actors did not care much for working in London, with bombs raining down. The music too was chosen with the utmost care and two songs were specially composed by Benjamin Britten. Yet, in spite of their excellence, they still might have been missed by thousands but for the fuss made by the Lord's Day Observance Society, whose present secretary says,

. . . the objection which the Society felt, in common with many other Christians, was that the play was irreverent and treated our Lord in a manner which to those who have a personal knowledge of Him as Saviour was most objectionable and hurtful. I must confess that the offence now seems somewhat mild compared with the excesses to which modern playwrights have gone in relation to our Lord Jesus Christ, but probably the milder incidents, such as that of Miss Sayers' play, were the beginning of the outrageous exhibitions in this field which we witness today. I feel, therefore, that the Society's protests in those days . . . were fully justified by subsequent events.

One cannot but agree that without *The Man Born to Be King* we should never have reached *Jesus Christ Superstar* via *Godspell,* and if you believe, as does the Lord's Day Observance Society, that it is the first step that leads to disaster, then they were within their rights to protest, but I think they might have waited until they had read the scripts, and not taken their cue from an inflammatory newspaper headline. *Jesus Christ Superstar* and *Godspell* speak to the people of today, and if Dorothy could have foreseen this outcome of her own work it is doubtful if, even then, she would have drawn back from the assignment. What were probably her last words on the subject came in 1953, when discussion of commercial television was in the air.

I will not permit, while I live, a teleview of "The Man Born to Be King" punctuated by advertisements. Though of course, it offers scope; the episode of the Feeding of the Five Thousand, presented by Hovis bread and MacFisheries for instance, would be very suitable.

10

War Efforts

Paradoxical as it may seem, to believe in youth is to look backward; to look forward we must believe in age. All normal children (however much we discourage them) look forward to growing up. "Except ye become as little children", except you can wake on your fiftieth birthday with the same forward-looking excitement and interest in life that you enjoyed when you were five, "ye cannot enter the kingdom of God". One must not only die daily, but every day one must be born again.

Dorothy L. Sayers, "Strong Meat" (essay)

Sometime during the Second World War, Dorothy gave up the flat in Great James Street, and she and Mac moved permanently to Witham. Until 1943 the bulk of her time was taken up with *The Man Born to Be King* and its repeats. She did a great deal of lecturing, and wrote several pamphlets—a type of publication which seems to have gone right out of fashion nowadays, except for specialized bodies who bring out their own treatises. It seems now like a waste of the wartime paper ration to put forth booklets, selling at threepence each, with such titles as *War with Honour* by A. A. Milne, *Nazi and Nazarene* by Ronald Knox and *Open Letter of an Optimist* by Hugh Walpole. One wonders who bought them, but they must have been of some profit to Macmillan, who published them. Dorothy's contribution was *The Mysterious English*, a study of the English character. She is scathing about the

semi-intellectuals, that curious little cosmopolitan crowd who have lost their English roots and wish to persuade us that Englishry is the last infirmity of the Blimpish mind. It cannot be said of them that:

> "Their voice is heard through rolling drums
> That beat to battle where they stand."

Some of them indeed, made no attempt to stand, but fled to the States while the going was good, where no doubt they are informing the trustful Americans that they have nothing to hope for from the British Navy.

This is a somewhat spiteful reference to Auden and one or two others who decided they would be more useful as live poets than dead soldiers and removed themselves to America when war first broke out. In actual fact none of them, through various physical disabilities, would have been accepted by any of the armed forces. The howl against them was vicious and it is sad to see one of Dorothy's standing joining in, especially as she was so enraged by the hounding of Wodehouse later on. Dorothy was intensely patriotic, in the old empire-builder's style, but, for a woman so gifted, strangely naïve about politics. She was ahead of her time in working for church unity, admitting that in every church there was *something* of God, but in politics she could see no shades, just black and white, or rather red and blue. The shock of the outcome of the 1945 election was for her, personally traumatic; and until the complexion of the government changed in 1951 she considered herself to be living under a tyranny. But if she failed to understand *party* politics, she had a wide understanding of the politics of life. As early as January 1940 she published a long essay, "Begin Here," setting forth how we should conduct ourselves, and prepare for the peace which would eventually come. Writing about economic man and science she says:

Science has placed in our hands methods by which the stubborn earth can be made to yield abundance for all its inhabitants—enough food, enough clothing, enough shelter for every man, woman and child in the world. There is no longer any real reason why anybody should go short; we know how to build in spots that seemed formerly inaccessible, how to combat diseases which used in former days to destroy whole civilisations. If there is a temporary shortage in one district, we know how to transport all our requirements quickly from districts in which there is a good provision of them. The control is ours, only we do not know how to use it. We see people so surfeited with luxuries that they are sunk in the physical, mental and spiritual cloth of mere glut tony—they literally do not know what to do with their possessions; side by side with them are slums, poverty and undernourishment, sometimes extending to whole peoples. At one spot we find town-dwellers forced to pay prohibitive prices for fish or fruit; while at another apples rot in the orchards and fish are used for manure, because the cost of their transport to town makes their sale a dead loss to fisherman and farmer. We have planters forbidden to grow rubber or cotton that their land would reasonably yield, because there is a hitch in the distribution of rubber or cotton manufactured goods; and we have at the same time greedy over-production of crops that robs the soil of nature and nurture, or reckless deforestation of great tracts of country, leading to droughts and floods and the destruction of life and property. One does not need to be an economist or an agriculturalist to know that such contrasts are monstrous and that such wanton ill-treatment of the earth and its products is both wicked and wasteful.

This could have been written by any dyed-in-the-wool socialist, and the final chapter of the book would not shame a Labor Party manifesto, yet she would have been outraged if anyone had suggested she was anything but the bluest of Tories. Much of her writing is so in tune with today's thought that it is sometimes difficult to remember that she was speaking nearly forty years ago. To quote again from "Begin Here":

The violent assertions of man's right to his animal nature which we find in many modern writers, and in the theories of those educationalists who demand complete self-expression (even if it manifests itself in kicking one's pastors and masters or taking off all one's clothes in public), are a revolt against past systems of thought which repressed

Biological Man. Like most revolts, they tend to go too far in the other direction and create an "absolutism" of their own.

In an article, "The Human-Not-Quite-Human," which was written as a radio talk but rejected by the B.B.C. because "our listeners do not want to be admonished by a woman," she discusses the man/woman war, as lucidly and much more wittily than any present-day women's libber.

Probably no man has ever troubled to imagine how strange his life would appear to himself if it were unrelentingly assessed in the terms of his maleness; if everything he wore, said, or did had to be justified by reference to female approval; if he were compelled to regard himself, day in day out, not as a member of society, but merely (salva reverentia) as a virile member of society. If the centre of his dress consciousness were the codpiece, his education directed to making him a spirited lover and meek paterfamilias; his interests held to be natural only in so far as they were sexual. If from school and lecture-room, Press and pulpit he heard the persistent outpouring of a shrill and scolding voice bidding him remember his biological function. If he were vexed by continual advice how to add a rough male touch to his typing, how to be learned without losing his masculine appeal, how to combine chemical research with seduction, how to play bridge without incurring the suspicion of impotence.

His newspaper would assist him with a "Men's Corner" telling him how he could attract the girls and retain his wife's affection. People would write books called, "History of the Male" or "Psychology of the Male" or "Males of the Bible", and he would be regaled daily with headlines, such as "Gentleman Doctor's Discovery", and "Men Artists at the Academy". If he gave an interview to a reporter, he would find it recorded in such terms as these: "Professor Bract, although a distinguished botanist, is not in any way an unmanly man. He has, in fact, a wife and seven children; when I swilled beer with him in his laboratory, he bawled his conclusions at me in a strong gruff voice that implemented the promise of his swaggering moustache." Or: "I asked M. Sapristi, the renowned chef, whether kitchen-cult was not a rather unusual occupation for a man. 'Not a bit of it!' he replied, bluffly. 'It is the genius that counts, not the sex!' As they say in La belle Écosse, a man's a man for 'a that—and his gusty, manly guffaw blew three small patty pans from the dresser."

This talk is so full of wit and common sense that it would be an act of grace by the B.B.C. (still largely male dominated) if they recalled their yesterdays and had it broadcast now.

In her first year at Oxford Dorothy had daringly posed as an agnostic, and the bitter years of the early twenties had sorely tried her faith. Before *The Man Born to Be King,* she had written and talked very little about religion; she was not given to pious religious observance, although she went fairly regularly to church. When a writer becomes known for a particular kind of work, the public are apt to look upon him as an oracle upon the subject in question. Thus, a person brought up in the circus may write a very good book or play based on his own experiences; he is then looked upon as an expert on *everything* about the circus, and finds himself willy-nilly becoming such an expert, because he is always having to find answers to the questions put to him. So it was with Dorothy and religion—the more she wrote about it, the more religious she became. She was forever the great seeker, and she liked nothing more than a good theological discussion. Somewhere there must be hundreds of her letters written to various people on religious questions, and it may be that one day they will be collected together. It might be apposite to include here parts of two letters she wrote to Dr. Welch in November 1943, because she says for herself what she is getting at better than any paraphrase can do.

Dr. Welch had been taken to task by a listener about a radio sermon he had given. Dorothy writes:

This morning, after reading your letter, I was getting my breakfast when I had a sudden illumination! It must have been genuine, because the Devil, seeing it come into my mind, was so angry that he overthrew the coffee-pot (which was standing all by itself on the stove, doing no harm to anybody) and poured a pint and a half of freshly-made coffee over the gas-grill and the floor and into a small pan of fish cakes which I was in the act of frying. However, he got nothing by it except a little bad language.

This was it:

The moment the Devil sees that somebody may be really going to preach the Gospel, he puts it into their heads to announce that a Challenge has been issued to the Churches. Instantly everybody's attention is diverted from the Gospel and focused on the Challenger, the Churches, the Preachers, the B.B.C., Christendom, Organized Religion, the Need for a More Spiritual Outlook, the Social Crisis or anything else that usefully pushes God into the background.

Blow (if I may put it that way) the challenge to your preaching at the microphone! Whatever you do, don't suggest publicly that you have been challenged. Everybody is only too anxious to rush in and criticise and agree that the whole trouble with Christianity is bad preaching. Nothing will delight the Devil more than to see them all chasing after this beautiful stuffed electric hare. The minute you say you have been challenged *you* step into the centre of the picture, and everybody dismisses God from their minds to take a good, satisfying look at Broadcasting House. . . .

Never mind the challenging letters from clever listeners. It will only fix people's minds on the writer of the letter ("so striking") and on you answering it ("so courageous"). After all, you and I and the Radio Padre and the Archbishop and Uncle Tom Cobley and all are of the utmost insignificance. You don't want the listeners to look on at a dogfight— you want them to look at Christ. Tell them who God is, and what He does and did. Tell them God was crucified, and that they have got to be crucified too. (Because that's what they want to know—they want to know that their suffering makes sense. And it's no good saying they can't understand it, they've *got* to understand it, that's what it's all about.) Challenges to the Church don't matter a hoot. . . . The important thing is the mutual challenge between God and Man.

Just go and preach the Gospel at the Market Cross. Never mind the wigs and gloves on the green—the Devil only throws them there to divert people's attention. He doesn't mind *what* they look at so long as it isn't the Cross.

This letter has a postscript twice as long as itself which is a discussion of the Godhead of Christ and man's inability to understand the meaning of the redemption of sin. She returns to this point in the second letter written ten days later.

. . . the "story" of Crucified God appears irrelevant because people nowadays have no sense of sin. . . . I'm a very poor person to appreciate modern man's feelings in all this, because I can't think of any personal misfortunes which have befallen me which were not, in one way or another, my own fault. I don't mean this necessarily in the profounder and more religious sense, I mean that I know jolly well that if anything unpleasant has happened to me in my life, I had usually "asked for it". Consequently, when I talk about carrying the sins of the world, "I'm going outside my experience—anything I have to put up with looks to me like the direct punishment for my *own* sins, and not to leave much margin over for the redemption of other peoples". But I do see that most people do look upon themselves as the victims of undeserved misfortunes, which they have done nothing to provoke, Contemporary literature and thought seem to be steeped in self-pity, which is the most enervating state of mind imaginable.

If only they could start from the idea that there is "something funny about man"—and that he does tend to fight against the right order of things, they could get a more robust outlook on suffering and catastrophes, and see that they were carrying:

a) the direct consequence of their wrongness—the "punitive element" in suffering

b) the indirect consequence of other people's wrongness—the "redemptive" element . . .

I remember Alan Wheatley saying "I can't bear all this killing—it's so *irrevocable*". All death is irrevocable, that's why we find it such an outrage. . . . There isn't any "escape" or "fresh start" in the sense of *abolishing* the past and its consequences. The past can never be wiped out, but only redeemed and "made good". To *escape* from the past would mean Christ coming down from the Cross; to redeem the past means going through the Cross to the Resurrection. One muddle about forgiveness is of the same kind—forgiveness is the restoration of a good relationship, but it doesn't abolish the consequence of the offence, nor is it going back to where we were before the offence was committed, it's got to be a new relationship. . . . If I borrow money from you and squander it, your forgiving the debt doesn't put back the money—that's lost, and you bear the loss and so "carry the guilt". If I get in a rage with you and throw your best teapot out of the window, no amount of forgiveness will unbreak the teapot—all we can aim for is a relationship in which both you *and* I can bear to sit down and breakfast together out of a shaving mug without feeling uncomfortable and without an ostentatious avoidance of the subject of teapots. . . .

I think it's here that the relevancy of the Cross comes in—that the power which made and sustains the Universe, with its iron laws is the Power that (not prevents evil from happening, which would make freedom of choice unmeaning, but) makes evil good. . . .

Dorothy was working at a very high pitch during the whole of the war. Money was an ever-present worry; there was the child's education, which had reached its most expensive stage, and various other calls on her purse from elderly and needy relatives. Mac was earning nothing, and was retreating more and more to the bottle. He was in his sixties, his looks faded, but some vestiges of his great charm were left. He was not particularly happy; Dorothy was so often away, and he was lonely. It is strange that with the military reputation he had built up for himself he did not join the Home Guard; but he seems to have contented himself by recounting tales "of battles long ago" in the pub across the road. When Dorothy was at home there were frequent rows with the domestic staff, who would then walk out and leave them in the lurch. Much of Dorothy's correspondence is punctuated with excuses about the paucity of her maids and cooks, but I have heard from some of her staff who worked for her for years, and were very happy in the household. It is possible they were sometimes used as excuses for unmet deadlines, and of course during the war the whole relationship was changed. Ladies "obliged," and they were no longer maids. Dorothy had been brought up in houses teeming with domestics, and her parents had always been well served, not least because the Reverend Henry had paid rather more than the going rate for the time. Dorothy had inherited the housekeeper from Christchurch rectory when her father died, and when she left to be married she was followed by a young couple who stayed for five and a half years; the wife has given a picture of the household in her day.

Miss Sayers' day started at 7.45; she would have her bath, read her mail, then breakfast, tea and toast at 8.30. I would go in for the tray at 9 o'clock and we would settle the day's menu. Everything was good plain cooking, and I did all my own baking; they liked good food and plenty of it.

Lunch was at 1 o'clock, light tea 4.15 and dinner at 8.

Miss Sayers was a large woman and always wore a suit, silk blouse, tie and cuff links, very smart. When she went out she wore a hat, something like an artist wears, and a brown flowing cloak—people used to turn and look at her. She was very nice to everybody. I had £5 a week housekeeping, just for milk, greengrocer, window cleaner and the woman who washed and ironed every week and for odds and ends; all large bills were paid monthly. We were the first married couple they had, and our wage was £1 15s. a week, but we lived well, had a nice bedroom, bathroom and sitting room.

After her breakfast she would go to her library and write; if she had a problem she would walk for hours back and forth in the garden. I don't know if I should say this, but Major Fleming was very fond of the bottle, and sometimes Miss Sayers would ask me to make up the spare bed, and she would say "one of those days". She knew we knew, but we never spoke about them outside. When the major was all right, a nicer man you couldn't find. He used to come into the kitchen, and talk to me, and ask for a coffee, and wanted me to have it with him, which I did, and we would talk about all sorts of things.

I had my son while we were there. Miss Sayers did not want us to leave, and did she think I could cope? I said I'd try. She got me a daily woman two months before, and she stayed two months after, and she [Miss Sayers] thought I managed very well. We left four years after when my daughter was on the way.

A more kind, thoughtful person never lived, and I was very sorry when she died.

The houses at Witham (for she took in the one next door when Aunt Maud came to settle with her) were nothing more than cottages, to which at some time a false Georgian front had been added. They opened almost directly onto the street, and all the rooms were extremely small. With two families, one including a baby, to say nothing of the aunt and her parrot, a cinema next door, and a parking lot up against the front windows, all on the main road to London, the place can hardly have resembled a writer's retreat. There was a large garden but even so it cannot have been a very peaceful establishment, and Dorothy was never able to get staff to stay very long after the married couple left. She does not seem to have had her father's generosity with regard to wages, which she was apt to forget to pay, and never seemed to realize that for a domestic to have to ask for money constituted an insult. Although she had a mind as well ordered as a computer, she was, in her habits, extremely untidy. Her study was a shambles, and her bedroom looked like a drapers after the sales had struck. Her attitude toward money was monarchial; she hardly ever carried it with her but always paid by check and signed the bills in restaurants. As she grew older she got worse in this respect, and this may have been the cause of much of the friction between herself and the domestic staff.

In spite of Mac's reputation as a cook and the fact that he dedicated his book, *Gourmet's Book of Food and Drink,* "To my wife who can make an omelette," I have found no one who remembers him actually cooking. It was always Dorothy who did that—superbly, according to her friends, and in 1951 she threatened to give up writing altogether and to hire herself out as "a good plain cook." Could it be that it was she who drafted the *Gourmet* articles for Mac to put together?

After the excitement of *The Man Born to Be King* came the inevitable emptiness. Dr. Welch suggested she should do for St. Paul what she had done for Christ, but St. Paul did not catch her imagination. She also said no to the Old Testament. "I am hopelessly allergic to Old Testament characters, and besides I don't really know enough O.T. history." In August 1943 she told Val Gielgud she had "at last got an idea for *your* play—if it works, an episode from Froissart—*Mechanism of Treason".*

She mentioned this idea to several people, but apparently it did not work for it was never completed. She should have been making quite a good income in spite of the calls upon her. The Wimsey books were still selling well, *The Man Born to Be King* was translated and broadcast worldwide, and there were her lectures and translations. It is true that the B.B.C. fees had slipped from their early heights, but it was steady money, and, as important, instant. Val Gielgud produced *Whose Body?* in six parts, for which a fee of twenty guineas an episode was offered. Someone at the B.B.C. thought this was too low, and spontaneously offered to raise the price to twenty-four guineas an episode. Dorothy, however, refused the new rate on the grounds that she had already signed the contract, and thus accepted the original offer, which, if she really was short of money, was sticking to a principle with a vengeance.

Dorothy did not concern herself with war work as such, except for knitting socks for trawlermen from thick, coarse wool. She kept chickens and a pig to help out with the rations. The pig was called Francis Bacon and had the run of the house as well as the garden. Once, after sitting on one side of the fireplace with her knitting, Mac on the other with his paper, she went out to put the kettle on for tea. Francis Bacon wandered in and tangled his trotters with the knitting wool. Mac, waking from a light doze behind his newspaper, thought he saw his wife transformed into a pig. It was a much-loved animal, the subject of foolish endearments and all manner of cosseting—but they ate him. A typical example of Dorothy's ability to shut doors on life. There was no connection, once the deed of slaughter was done, between the bacon on the plate, and the affectionate creature that had come at her call and chuntered round the house like a happy if somewhat feeble-minded child.

Witham did not escape occasional air raids and unexploded bombs. Dorothy made no attempt to hide the fact that these terrified her and she always retreated to the cellar with her knitting at the first pip of the air-raid warning, leaving Mac grumbling in the garden because the "Hun buggers were too hidden by clouds to be seen." Worse than the ordinary air raids were the V1 missiles which, if they missed London, carried on over the southern part of Essex and spent themselves harmlessly for the most part in the open country. The sound of these things going overhead and the terror that seized everyone when the engine cut out frightened even Mac, and *he* would be then the one to hustle everyone into the cellar.

But it was to one of these V1 missiles that we owe the Sayers translation of Dante.

11

And So to Dante

Any translator of Dante is nowadays in an awkward position. Hundreds of translations have already appeared—in
prose, in blank verse, in terza rima, in blank terza rima, in
octosyllabic terza rima, in heroic couplets, in Spenserian
stanzas, in Marvellian quatrains, and I know not what besides. If he supposes he is going to surpass all his predeces-
sors, he is in danger of appearing a presumptuous ass. If he
modestly admits that he cannot surpass them, then he *is* a
presumptuous ass—since what reason, except an overween-
ing personal vanity, can he possibly have for demanding
that the world should buy and read an inferior version
which has no recommendation except that it is his.
Dorothy L. Sayers, "The Poetry of Search and the Poetry
of Statement"

Mac was yelling from the top of the cellar steps, "Come on
Dorothy! Doodlebugs!" She had been searching for something
in her desk, scattering papers behind her as a rabbit throws up
earth when burrowing, and had not heard the devilish grinding
roar from above. At the sound of Mac's warning, and the air-raid
siren, she rushed downstairs, grabbing the first book her hand
encountered, for she always, wherever she went, *had* to have
something to read. Only when she was seated in the cellar did
she realize that the book she had picked up was an old volume

of Dante in the original medieval Italian. She was slightly annoyed as she did not know even modern Italian but she found
that, with her Latin and French, she could make a good deal of
sense of *The Divine Comedy*. By the time the "all clear"
sounded, she was hooked.

For years Charles Williams had tried to get Dorothy interested in Dante, but she had always been busy with something
else, and put off by what she thought would be a language
difficulty. Charles Williams and C. S. Lewis were the most popular writers on religious questions in the thirties. Dorothy corre-
sponded with both of them, though these letters have not yet
come to light, and they formed themselves into a kind of loosely
knit club, referring to themselves as the Inklings because they
thought they each had a glimpse of the meaning of God. C. S.
Lewis, with his *Screwtape Letters* and fairy tales for children, is
still read. Charles Williams, however, seems to be in eclipse.
Dorothy was still broadcasting, overseeing amateur productions of her plays, and writing articles, but she had no big work
on hand. The straight novel she had for so long promised Gollancz was refusing to be written, and her Froissart idea was
eluding her. Then, suddenly, came the brainwave. Why not a
new translation of Dante? Not Dante for scholars, but for the
ordinary non-classically-educated English reader, the sort of
thing that Dr. E. V. Rieu was doing with his Penguin editions
of the classics. First, though, she had to teach herself Italian, and
read the previous translations of the *Comedy*, of which there
were many. "When I wanted to work on Dante, I taught myself
to read the mediaeval Italian in a very few weeks' time, with
the aid of Latin, an Italian grammar, and the initial assistance
of a crib," she told an audience during a lecture on the teaching
of Latin. She was now in her fifty-second year, with two careers,
as a detective story writer and as a religious playwright, behind
her. Most people so circumstanced would quail at the prospect
of striking out in another new direction, one which was to bring

her into head-on clashes with scholars, who considered her action one of effrontery, and to cause outcries from those still
thirsty for more Wimsey books. It would take a great deal of
time and expense to do the necessary research, and the reward,
even if she succeeded in artistic terms, would be financially
minimal. Also it was a pretty crowded field; the best known
translation at the time was Binyon's, with which most people
were satisfied.

Nothing anybody could say to her would make Dorothy draw
back from the project which had fired her imagination and
which she *needed* to do, since she thought the world was waiting for a new *Divine Comedy*. Although she often quoted Disraeli's dictum "Never excuse, never explain," it was not one she
followed herself. She was always excusing and explaining why
she was doing this work, to say nothing of explaining Dante
himself. "No translation of any great classic can ever in the
nature of things be definitive," she wrote, "for each one necessarily takes some colour from the age in which it is written, and
to that extent falsifies its original."

By early 1945 she felt ready to suggest the project to Dr. Rieu.

Blank verse I believe to be the most hopeless of all forms of Dante. It
has none of the movement, and it makes it far too easy to be literal and
timid; so that all you get is something that might have been good prose
if it hadn't been hammered and twisted into ten-syllable lines. It had
to be either prose or the original verse-form; and here, you see, I
succumbed to the terrible fascination of struggling with the *terza rima*
—a form to which the English language is said not to take kindly,
owing to the scarcity of rhyme-sounds and the still greater scarcity of
feminine endings. But the fun of this kind of thing *is* the difficulty.
. . . I have also taken liberties with the metre which would make the
hair of 18th or 19th century translators stand up on their heads—but
in that, I am nearer to Dante than they are, since (allowing for the
elisions and so on) I have personally counted no fewer than seventeen
syllables in one of his lines.

No translation of Dante can be perfect; but if one is to shove in with a new version at this time of day, I suppose one ought to be able to claim to have done something or other which earlier translators have missed. . . . I think the trouble with all of them is that they have far, far too much reverence for their author. They are afraid to be funny, afraid to be undignified; they insist on being noble and then end by being prim. But prim is the one thing Dante never is . . . you are astonished (at least, I was astonished) to meet delicate Dante, homely Dante, and even dear, funny Dante, always a little mocking at himself as he is dragged and scolded and chivvied from circle to circle, staggering between a paralysing personal timidity and a "satiable curiosity" which would do credit to any Elephant's Child. . . .

Whether I've at all succeeded in "getting" the Dante I find in the poem is another matter—but that's the Dante I'm trying to get. You may think the result quite awful. . . . I agree with you about liking the "Purgatorio" best—that's one reason why I didn't begin with it: on the principle of the indignant father with the suitor who boasted of the chastity of his life: "My God Sir! have you the infernal impudence to suggest that you should try your prentice hand on my daughter?" . . . In the meantime if you have a copy of Binyon handy, I wish you would have a look at him. He is . . . the most modern of the verse translators, and an established poet. He is much more accurate and reverent than I am; all I can say for myself is that I think my version is livelier—my leopard more prettily spotted, my loathsome worms more loathsome, my whirlwind whizzier, my frogs squelchier and my Inferno, generally speaking "louder and funnier."

The work was accepted and Dorothy spent the next three years on *Inferno*, while at the same time writing the Lichfield play and mapping out *The Emperor Constantine*. She wrote several articles on Dante, and in 1946 was invited by Barbara Reynolds, who was secretary to the Society for Italian Studies, to speak in Cambridge at a summer school.

Barbara Reynolds had seen a notice of the forthcoming translation of Dante by Dorothy L. Sayers, and thought at least her name would be a draw. Foreign travel was still restricted in England, so that the summer school drew a great many more students than it would otherwise have done. People interested in Italy were thirsty for news of a country that had been closed

to them for the long war years, and avid to speak Italian together. Dorothy's lecture, in the great hall of Jesus College, was
entitled "The Eighth Bolgia," and over two hundred people
crowded in to hear it. It went, as they say, "like a bomb," for
she made Dante *live* as no one had ever done before. The
liveliness was highlighted by the arid readings given by a
professor in Italian of extracts to illustrate the lecture. Dorothy
looked down sideways at him as he droned on, dying, no doubt,
to say "That is what I mean by burying Dante in scholarship,"
but she desisted. This summer school marked the beginning of
a friendship between Barbara Reynolds and Dorothy which
lasted for the rest of Dorothy's life.

Long before the first part of the trilogy was published there
were articles in the press denigrating the work in progress. It
seemed that Dorothy was again to be condemned without trial,
as had happened with *The Man Born to Be King.*

"Here is an outburst from the *Irish Press,*" she wrote to Rieu
on December 12, 1947.

Let me have it back sometime, because it gives me profound pleasure.
At the back of it, of course, is the profound uneasiness which Dante
nearly always arouses in post-Tridentine R.C.s, coupled with their
peevish jealousy that anyone else should presume to understand him.
. . . But most exquisitely naïve of all is the notion that one must wait
for a version of Dante (or whatever) until a poet as great as Dante
comes along to do it. Poets of that calibre are rare; and when they do
come along, they usually want to write poems of their own, not translate other people's. Moreover, the new Dante might not know either
English or Italian—or he might (horrible dictu) be a Protestant or an
atheist. . . . It is true that a new comet was seen this week; but even
if it heralds the birth of this phenomenon he will scarcely be ready to
do the job before we are all too old.

That Dante was the last love of her life is evident from the
great pains she took, not only with the translation, but also with
the verification of every fact, studying medieval astronomy and
so forth, and even with the actual layout of the books.

I have based my rough lay-outs on 12 terzains to the full page. If you are setting in 10-point, this is probably as much as you can cram in. If I can trust the rather imprecise instruments I have at hand, it might be *just* possible to squeeze in 13 to the page, by using only a ¼ em lead between the stanzas, but there would be an impasse if a line over-ran. In 9-point you could probably get the 13 terzains to the page, and then we should have loads of elbow-room; but it would be better to have the text set as big as possible.

She asks for forgiveness for

incursion into the printer's domain. Two years in the publishing and nine years in the advertising have left me with an inclination to stick my nose into lay-out. But if I am babbling, pay no attention!

She was not babbling. The printers and editors knew a professional when they saw one, and the books were printed in accordance with her many detailed suggestions.

In 1946 came George Bernard Shaw's ninetieth birthday and the sudden death of H. G. Wells, two events which sent publishers and printers right off course; as she wrote to an American friend:

I am having great fun with Dante, though irritated at the moment by a prolonged hold-up over specimen pages, for which I have been waiting now, more or less patiently, for nearly six months. The excuse offered is a) congestion in the printing trade owing to lack of labour; b) the fact that all the labour there was has been put on to celebrating Bernard Shaw's 90th birthday with festal volumes. And now, I suppose, it is going to be put on to celebrating the death of H. G. Wells with memorial volumes. So that Dante and I fall between two stools—I being only in my fifties, and he being already six hundred years dead —and cannot compete in the struggle to attract public attention. However, I daresay we shall get only too much of it when we do succeed in getting published, for I shall offend all the scholars and all the Dante-devotees by insisting on treating him as a superb story teller with a lively sense of humour instead of as a superhuman sourpuss steeped to the eyebrows in grimth.

She was less lighthearted with Penguin over this holdup and begged Dr. Rieu to remind his staff "that there is a Vestibule in Hell, in which persons unable to bring themselves to any decision run perpetually, stung by wasps and hornets."

Dr. Rieu and others continued to be bombarded with letters about the lay-out almost up until the day of publication; the smallest thing would set her off, not only into prose, but into verse as well:

> And now I tune my brazen throat
> To sing in harsh, emphatic strain
> With what abhorrence, rage and pain
> I contemplate the SINGLE QUOTE.

I hate it. For one thing the eye slips over it too easily (especially when it is combined with the beastly modern habit of insufficiently indenting the beginning of a paragraph) and may easily miss it altogether. Dante is difficult enough already, without our conspiring to prevent people from seeing where dialogue ends and narrative begins. . . . Never mind your house-rule or look of the page—we want to be intelligible.

Moreover, I think the Single Quote is ugly in itself. It looks an ass if it comes up against a final apostrophe and it looks a thundering ass when it comes to quotes within quotes. A mimsy little pale Single Quote trying to enclose a fat black Double Quote reminds me of negro baby whose woollies have shrunk in the wash.

The first Dante volume, which she insisted should be called *Hell*—"a good English word"—came out in 1949 to a storm of disapproval. Not because *someone* had dared to re-translate Dante, but because that someone was Dorothy L. Sayers. For the second time in her life she had stepped out of the pigeonhole into which the public had put her. One would have thought, from the scholarly hands wrung in horror, that Dorothy had presumed to do this work having scarcely mastered her A-B-Cs. Anyone would have been annoyed at the sheer stupidity of her critics, and Dorothy was naturally, enraged, as she wrote to Rieu:

I enclose a copy of *Tristan in Brittany*, because I don't think I made myself very clear on the telephone about the title and author of the

poem. I think you ought just to mention this job—I really do. Especially
if you are going to hammer in the point (which *I* feel it better not to
insist on) that it is only recently that I "fell in love", with Dante. It is,
in the long run, not good for your Penguins, as it is certainly not good
for my reputation to encourage the idea (with which papers like the
"New Statesman" are only too happy to make play) that I am merely
a middle-aged sensation-novelist amateurishly dabbling in this or that
gigantic project, without training or qualifications. If I have not been
long a Dantist, I am at least a Romance linguist and, to some extent,
a mediaevalist. I was a scholar of my college, I am a Master in my
University; I took First-class Honours, and was, after all, a scholar and
poet before I was anything else.

Though I find some amusement in the impertinences of the Press,
I do not altogether relish them. It is not true that I have "turned from
popular fiction to take up" a pretentious high-browism; I am going on
from where I began, after twenty years at the money-making mill of
fiction. I would not have the insolence to touch Dante if I were what
the reviewers make me out to be. It is true that in theology I am
self-trained; but I am not without the fundamental equipment which
makes self-training possible. I *will* not have my qualifications for this
particular job supposed to rest upon a glib tongue, a facile pen, and a
knack of concocting "thrillers". All these things help to make scholarship palatable to the masses. But I *have* received "licentium incipiendi
in facultate Artium legendi, disputandi, et caetera omnia fasciendi
quae ad statum Magistri in aedem facultate pertinent", and there are
moments when I would rather not be wholly cheapened for the delight
of those who hate learning. . . .

The upshot of this is that I think we owe it to Dante, if not to myself,
to make clear a) that this is not my first attempt at translating from a
mediaeval text; b) that I have sufficient scholarship and academic
standing to make the present venture not altogether impertinent;
c) that I do not myself consider the writing of popular novels and radio
plays in itself a qualification for translating and editing the "Divine
Comedy". I do not want to stand upon my dignity, but if you do not
allow me just a *little* dignity I shall look a greater fool even than I am.

It is certainly possible that the reader without formal classical
or literary training can learn more about theology, medieval
history, and Renaissance Italy from Dorothy L. Sayers's Dante

than from any other source. Her introductions and notes alone are more informative than another's scholarly treatise. As to the poetry, how much of it is Sayers and how much Dante, I am unable to judge, but I do know I was chilled by

> No cask stove in by cant or middle ever
> So gaped as one I saw there, from the chin
> Down to the fart-hole split as by a cleaver.

> His tripes hung by his heels; the pluck and uploon
> Showed with the liver and the sordid sack
> That turns to dung the food it swallows in.

It is nasty, but so is Hell.

Some lines are, I feel, a little awkward, and the use of certain words questionable in the context. Dorothy said she had tried "to avoid the poles of 'quotha! and 'sez you!' " and I think it was a mistake to make a character in Purgatory speak in what she calls "Border-Scots" because the "dialect bears something of the same relation to English as Provençal does to Italian." It is never wise to write in Scots dialect if you happen not to be a Scot, and in this particular context the effect is dreadful. But some of the lines are beautiful, particularly the rendering of the Lord's Prayer by the penitent Proud in Purgatory. What probably annoyed the bookroom scholars was Dorothy's speed and fluency—they were, in fact, jealous. And they still are. *The Times Literary Supplement* of June 4, 1971, carried a long unsigned review of two new translations of Dante; various previous versions were mentioned, but not a word about Dorothy L. Sayers.

The task on which she had set out with so much enthusiasm in 1944 was becoming a chore by 1953. "Nobody I assure you, will be more rejoiced to see the back of the damn things than I shall!" By September of that year *Purgatory* was finished and published in 1955 to a booming silence from the scholastic world, which, seeing that she could not be stopped by calumny, pretended she was not there. She carried on with *Paradise* but had only completed twenty cantos when she died. The work was completed by Barbara Reynolds, following so accurately the terza rima style of Dorothy that, in theatrical parlance, "you can't see the join." Dr. Reynolds also followed Dorothy's method with the notes and commentaries, and Mr. Scott-Giles provided the maps and drawings, as he had done for the first two volumes.

It was a tragedy that Dorothy was unable to see the final outcome of her last great love affair; for it was that. As much as she had loved any man or friend, she loved Dante, and this love comes through her many articles and essays, through the hundreds of letters she wrote about the work in progress, through the work itself. Whatever its merits or demerits as a translation, a work of scholarship or a poem in its own right, it stands as a monument to this great love.

At the same time as she was working on Dante for the Penguin Classics series, Dorothy was preparing *The Song of Roland* for a King Penguin edition. Her hope was that Miss Pope, with whom she had first read Roland way back in 1912, and who thought her translation "showed some promise of distinction," would live to see it in print, but she died shortly before its publication in 1957.

12

🌱

Final Chapters

There is one vast human experience that confronts us so
formidably that we cannot pretend to overlook it. There is
no solution to death. There is no means whatever whereby
you or I, by taking thought, can solve this difficulty in such
a manner that it no longer exists.

Dorothy L. Sayers, *The Mind of the Maker*

In the spring of 1950 Mac had died, as inconsiderate with his
timing as he always was, for Dorothy was at her busiest, with
Dante, the Colchester Festival play, reviewing and lecturing.
He was in his seventieth year, and it was a long time since he
had been the center of her life. They had jogged along compan-
ionably enough towards the end, but his final going was little
more than a nuisance, an unwanted interruption, and eventually a release.

Funerals and cremations (especially) are a most wearing business, and
dealing with wills still worse, in that it goes on longer. These things are
probably quite good for some people in that they leave them no time
for brooding, but when one is already only too busy they seem to make
one's troubles almost unbearable.

There was no will to bother with so far as Mac was concerned,
and his few effects were soon disposed of. His casket stood

around for several weeks, for he had expressed a desire for his ashes to be scattered in a church in Lanarkshire, where most of his family were buried. It so happened that the local doctor at Witham came from that part of the world, and when he was going on holiday Dorothy asked him if he would take the urn along with him and "do the job." The doctor put all that was left of Mac in the trunk of his car and, arriving at the town, found that he had stopped his car most appropriately outside a public house called "The Fleming Arms." Feeling somewhat embarrassed, as if he were engaged in some nefarious pursuit, he wandered around the churchyard, fulfilling his peculiar mission, and then made off smartly to continue his holiday.

Dorothy shut the door of her mind on Mac and for the few years left to her hardly ever mentioned him. But the house was not the same without him. There was no one to curse her for her untidiness, to feed the cats, answer the telephone (and forget to pass on the messages) or to try out jokes on. She had always longed for the place to be quiet; with him there had always been some kind of noise—nagging when he was fretful, boisterously singing when he was cheerful, rambling during his increasingly frequent drunken spells, and snoring when he slept. Never was a place so full of a man as this small cottage was with Mac, and never so empty as when he departed. Whenever she could she stayed away, and but for the cats would probably have left it altogether.

Her attitude toward the press became even more ambivalent. On the one hand there was the "Miss Sayers never gives interviews" stance, which is contradicted by the number of items appearing in the newspapers about her, and her frequent dashes into the correspondence columns. One reporter had an alarming experience when he was sent to interview her about the Colchester Festival play. As he was being ushered to the drawing room, she, on hearing him approach, had risen to stir the fire, so that his first view of the lady was of an enormous behind. She whirled around, poker in hand, demanded "Are you a Christian?" and then proceeded to lecture him for over an hour on the Trinity.

Another reporter was castigated for saying that her hobbies were cats and gardening.

I do not see why anybody should want to know my hobbies—but if they do it would surely be better to mention the right ones. The choice was peculiarly unfortunate. If there is anything I detest it is gardening; and although my household always includes a necessary cat, which lives in the kitchen, and is supposed to catch mice, I have little to do with it.

But she adored cats, wrote poems about them and even sent Christmas cards from "Bramble, Sandra, George and Tibby Tandrum." During the war she queued up personally for their food, in the same way as Dr. Johnson had done his own shopping for Hodge, because it was an indignity she did not wish to put on her servant. Moreover, she did this not only for her own cats —she managed to get some extra for Val Gielgud's Siamese. She may not have cared a great deal for gardening, but she was crazy about cacti, and had a greenhouse stuffed with them. Certainly her justification in complaining about press reports would have been even greater if she could have seen Nancy Spain's article in the *Daily Express* when she died. "A great shy, short-sighted hulk of a woman, cut off in her later years by deafness," bannered Miss Spain (herself no wraith). It is true Dorothy was large, and may have been deaf to Nancy, but certainly to no one else. Almost every other fact mentioned in the article was incorrect. When she was invited by the B.B.C. to contribute to a program called "Personal Call," Dorothy left it to her secretary to reply that "Miss Sayers will never speak to any headline which makes use of the words 'I' or 'My' or which introduces the 'personal approach' to any subject whatever." But one of the last articles she wrote—for the *Sunday Times*—was under the headline "My Belief About Heaven and Hell".

Dorothy also became very angry with those clergymen who asked her to open their fêtes.

How dare they talk about Christian vocation, when at the same time they try to take me away from my vocation, which is to be a craftsman with words, to waste my time doing something for which I have no vocation and no talent, merely because I have a name.

But there again, she *did* open fêtes, and sales of work, and she attended prize givings. She seemed to want it both ways—to have her work recognized and to retain her privacy. But part of the price of that recognition is to be a public figure and a public servant, and that she did not welcome. "If you can't stand the heat," said Harry S. Truman, "get out of the kitchen." Dorothy never got out of the kitchen; she did things—like making absurd pronouncements, writing letters to the newspapers, wearing outlandish clothes—all calculated to raise the heat, and then complained when she got singed.

Although Dorothy never disowned Wimsey, she refused to consider writing any more books about him, blaming the income tax authorities. In 1953 she approached Val Gielgud about radio plays because of her "accursed and ever shrinking bank balance." She was, she said, "in a cleft stick, between the wolf at the door and the income tax." Her position was, no doubt, that of many writers, who have to pay in their lean years for assessments made in their good years, and are forced to work hard on a project while in actual fact not earning any money, or rather any profit, at all. Since her day, writers and artists generally have had some relief in the way their taxes are levied, but it did not come in time to help Dorothy. When she died she left just over £34,000, which was minute when one considers the amounts she must have earned gross. As she lived comparatively modestly, and indulged in no outrageous extravagances—one has only to look at photographs of her, in which she appears to have worn the same costume for thirty years—it can only be assumed that the state benefited from her industry far more than she did. Val Gielgud put forward a suggestion that Giles Cooper should adapt *The Nine Tailors* as a serial, with which Dorothy was in agreement as long as "Peter Wimsey is played straight and really does sound like somebody (in the great Hanaud's phrase) 'out of the top of his drawers' and not like a caricature of Lord Haw-Haw in a comic paper. Get proper records of bell-ringing."

Dorothy was pleased about the honor awarded to Val's brother John—so suitable for a Shakespearean actor to be an Elizabethan knight—but her letters begin at this time to sound tired. Yet there was a spirited note to a producer: "I will kill them if they give my name as Dorothy Sayers. *She* is one of your own employees, and plays the ukulele or balalaika or something in music hall programmes." Her devouring interest in books continued and she was still reading almost everything that was published, except modern novels. When asked why she avoided these, she replied wearily,

> As I grow older and older
> And totter towards the tomb,
> I find that I care less and less
> Who goes to bed with whom.

Dorothy still had many friends, and with them she was as full of enthusiasm as ever, even when coping with burst pipes and leaking roofs and she-cats from nowhere who presented her with litters of kittens. She was flattered when the Essex Society of Change Ringers made her a life member, and overjoyed when the University of Durham conferred on her an Honorary Doctorate of Literature. The speech of the public orator at her installation begins a little flippantly for so august an occasion.

An examination of the claims of Miss Sayers to appear before us today must raise a preliminary doubt whether this is quite the sort of platform upon which she should be standing. The Documents in the Case, unobscured by Clouds of Witnesses, cannot be dismissed as Five Red Herrings in establishing this point. Long before the evidence for Unnatural Death, which had itself come out before Lord Peter viewed the Body, there could be no doubt Whose Body had been in question. In the Teeth of the Evidence, even after the Unpleasantness at the Bellona Club—and it will be remembered that this did not follow but preceded the notorious Gaudy Night—Miss Sayers publicly took the unfortunate view that a book called Murder Must Advertise had no personal application. As for her victim, before anyone could Have His Carcase, Strong Poison proved to be present: and it is my feeling that there would have been no need to cite the Nine Tailors or to take the case further had not the Hangman's Holiday intervened.

Here the joking stopped and the oration continued more seriously:

But Miss Sayers is an adept in triumphantly dispelling dark clouds of suspicion, and it may be fairly asserted that her detective novels have collectively given more pleasure to educated readers than any since Conan Doyle's immortal series. Both authors present the personality and circumstances of their characters so vividly that the accessory details sometimes count for even more than the main story. By this subtle means their stories become vehicles of their own attitude to society and its problems, material and moral: and a penetrating criticism of these matters is implanted in the guise of an idle tale.

This breadth of outlook and of human sympathy is well known to be in Miss Sayers the basis of a moral strength, in which a lively and uncompromising Christianity is the central core. At a given moment novels were laid aside in favour of an earlier interest in religious truth and this was expressed in a stream of stimulating essays and plays and at length in a vigorous and painstaking verse translation of Dante's "Inferno". We have in Miss Sayers not only an artist, but a moralist who uses her art to convey a message with passionate desire to make it tell. A doctorate of Letters now to be conferred upon her expresses our admiration of her art, gay or grave, and a deep regard for her sincerity.

Dorothy loved to be called Dr. Sayers. She bought herself a fur coat to celebrate the honor, and was seldom seen out of it thereafter.

Miss Sayers in characteristic pose, at a rehearsal of *Christ's Emperor*, 1952

During these last years Dorothy became more and more interested and involved in church work. In 1952 those scenes from *The Emperor Constantine* depicting the conference at Nicea were made into a separate play and presented at St. Thomas's Regent Street as *Christ's Emperor.* In that year, too, she became the vicar's warden at this church. With the rapid deterioration of the fabric of St. Thomas's, which had suffered a great deal of war damage, it was decided by the church authorities to close it and to unite the parish with St. Anne's, Soho, and St. Paul's, Covent Garden. Dorothy resisted the closure of St. Thomas, which she considered an outrage, but she was overruled. It was closed, and since her death has been completely destroyed. St. Anne's, apart from the tower, had vanished in the blitz early in the war, so that the only working church was St. Paul's. Dorothy was made a church warden there, and attended the parish council meetings with great regularity until her death. She would sometimes read the Epistle at communion services in her academic hood—again, not the sort of thing to do if you did not want publicity. It was through her insistence that the ruined nave of St. Anne's was cleared and turned into a fee-paying parking lot. The churchyard was also renovated and turned into a garden of rest. Dorothy's ashes are in the tower of St. Anne's, awaiting a more fitting resting place, and although there was a fund put aside for a memorial to her, this has not yet been accomplished. As long ago as 1943, Dorothy was one of the founders of St. Anne's House experimental center, a place for people to meet "without distinction of race, creed or political alliance," and she had contributed to the first course of lectures, "Christian Faith and Contemporary Culture." Many other famous writers and thinkers from all over the world came to St. Anne's House to lecture in the years that followed, a great number of them first approached by Dorothy. They included T. S. Eliot, Nevill Coghill, Dr. Werner Brock, and M. Gabriel Marcel. There were seminars and concerts, and religious dramas were performed at St. Thomas's. First productions of Christopher Fry's *A Sleep of Prisoners* and Ronald Duncan's *This Way to the Tomb* were among the new plays presented by the drama group. There was a weird incident when a revival of Dorothy's *Zeal of Thy House* was stopped by a "common informer," only heaven knows on what grounds this action was taken against that entirely religious work. A lady who was also connected with St. Anne's at this time remembers Dorothy:

There was an occasion when the re-organisation Committee of the Diocese was trying to pull down St. Anne's. Dorothy made a fighting speech about what a body of determined lay people could do. A Canadian girl in the audience said that the devil was working through the re-organisation committee, and the chairman of the meeting, a Bishop, said "If I had known that the purpose of this meeting was to insult the committee of which I am chairman, I should not have come." What I chiefly remember about her is her clothes, her large grey bloomers which were much in evidence, but my most cherished memory is of a study circle to which I had gone rather unwillingly. There were only two others, one being Dorothy. The circle was conducted by the brilliant and saintly Rev. Gilbert Shaw. He was talking about the place where science, theology and philosophy meet. Something about "my universe and your postage stamp". I was completely out of my depth. Occasionally one toe touched bottom. But I did not dare admit it. After a while Dorothy said "I'm afraid it is rather beyond me." She inspired great love in me. She was obviously brilliant, yet so kind and approachable.

Frequently she would stay behind after the lectures and "hold court, talking brilliantly in almost uninterrupted monologue, until the small hours of the morning, with a glass of wine on her knee," remembers another St. Anne's worker. She had never entered much into the life at Witham, and was in fact scarcely known in the town. Margery Allingham lived not far away, but they only met once or twice on the train. In the preface to *Mr. Campion's Lady,* the second Allingham omnibus, Miss Allingham writes of her difficulty in getting her hero married.

I was so irritated with him and so anxious to get on with my lovely new idea that I got tough and made up my mind to hit him over the head, take away his memory, get Amanda interested in someone else, and leave him to get on with it.

It was an arbitrary move but they were arbitrary days. I remember telling Dorothy Sayers what I was about one afternoon when we were sharing a railway compartment in the midst of an air raid going up to London from Witham. We had never hit it off before but she understood the predicament perfectly and the tactic amused her. She laughed and laughed and we became friends after that.

But not very close friends. Dorothy did get her to join the Detective Club where she remembered "swearing on a skull in front of Miss Dorothy Sayers, who was severe in a pince-nez and Mandarin coat." Dorothy would have been a great deal more severe if she had known Miss Allingham had deprived her of her "L."

Once Dorothy did address a Tory meeting at Witham during an election campaign, but it was anything but a successful affair. In her last years she kept no household staff, and could frequently be seen toddling down to the shops in an apron, the fur coat flung over her shoulders in cold weather.

Throughout the early fifties she was still contributing to broadcasting and organized two programs on Dante in which John Slater played the lead. Her interest in broadcasting was keen, and she always fancied herself as a broadcaster, though the professionals did not consider her to be very good at the microphone. She thought the B.B.C.'s Third Programme should be a place "where scholars might from time to time read a paper," and resented any suggestions about presentation from the producer. Of all the work she did for them the B.B.C. has retained only one imperfect disc, not especially recorded, but taken from the broadcast. From this it would seem that the

The writer, in a characteristically mannish costume and hat

professionals were right. There is little hint in it of the deep beauty of her voice which everyone remembers. It comes over flat and a bit monotonous, although the diction is very clear. It was impossible to correct disc recordings without damaging the record, so this one is left with the fluffs and coughs intact, and with the engineer's errors (it was faded out too quickly). But it is all there is of her solo, though there may be records of her in discussions with other people. Toward the end of 1955 she gave a series of talks at St. Thomas's on "Religion and Philosophy." The B.B.C. offered to repeat these on the air, but they wanted to use an actor to read the poetry extracts. Dorothy considered this insulting; she was, she said, quite capable of reading a few lines of verse, had in fact been reading verse all her life. Younger men were coming up in the B.B.C., those who were not awed by Miss Sayers's reputation. They refused to give in and withdrew the invitation. Dorothy had one last sulky fling at the "frivolity of the B.B.C.'s policy of having every incidental quotation of verse turned into a vaudeville act." It was a pity, for tape recording had by then been perfected, and if the talks had been done we should know a great deal more about her broadcasting ability. This was her last encounter with the corporation during her lifetime, but they have certainly done her proud since she died.

Dorothy was never an abstemious person. In her last years she overate to an alarming degree, and although she drank only wine, she was apt to do it to the verge of excess, though she was never at any time seen the worse for drink. Her weight increased so that walking became a difficulty. Frequently she went to stay with Barbara Reynolds in her quaint corner flat in Cambridge. Barbara and her husband, Lewis Thorpe, had two young children, and the only way they could accommodate a visitor was to put a bed up in the large Victorian bathroom. Dorothy found this arrangement highly amusing and "so convenient for all one's needs."

In mid-December 1957 she had gone to Cambridge to go over some of the text of *Paradise*. She insisted on going out into the crowded Saturday streets to look for a gramophone record for the young Thorpes' Christmas present. Barbara went with her, finding it difficult to keep her lively steps in tune with Dorothy's slow plodding. They talked about the children, and Barbara said her daughter had gone to Byron House School, and had been in a class taught by a Mrs. Whelpton. "She's the wife of a writer—Eric Whelpton." Dorothy stopped short and turned to stare in a shop window, fighting for composure; the name just tossed out after so many years had caught her unprepared. Barbara, who was at the time ignorant of the old story, was puzzled by Dorothy's sudden interest in motor mechanics' tools. They talked of children over the weekend, Dorothy expressing amazement for Barbara's interest in "these creatures with unformed minds," but always seeming to be on the verge of revealing something. Time and again she led the conversation up to a certain point, and then slid away. She went back to Witham and during the weekend entertained Val Gielgud to tea; he was interviewing her for the *Sunday Dispatch*, but she was never to see the article.

On Tuesday, December 17, she went up to London to do her Christmas shopping. In her usual way she chose gifts for her friends, leaving the shops to post them with her cards so that she had no parcels to carry. By the end of the day she felt very tired, and half thought of staying in town for the night; but then there were the cats to be fed, and she had asked Mr. Lapwood to meet her at Witham Station with his taxi. He noticed nothing unusual in her manner as she said goodnight to him at the front door. All she wanted to do was to have a bath and go to bed, but first, the cats must be seen to. She threw her bag and fur coat into the room which led off from the hall, and walked toward the kitchen; at the foot of the stairs, Death, about whom she had written so much, caught up with her, and she sank to the floor in a heap—untidy to the last. There Mrs. Wollage, her secretary, found her next morning.

It was ironic that she who had staged so many fictional post-mortems should have provided a real one herself. Death was from coronary thrombosis, which was what her doctor had predicted if she did not curb her appetite and chain-smoking. She had not cared; she feared most of all a lingering, humiliating dying; in this her God had not forgotten her. She would have loved her memorial service at St. Margaret's, Westminster. A panegyric written by C. S. Lewis was read by the Bishop of Chichester; also present were the bishops of Peterborough, Lichfield, Chelmsford, Kensington and Colchester. Perhaps she might have looked a little awry at the "Red" Dean of Canterbury, Dr. Hewlett Johnson, but certainly she would have appreciated the first lesson read by Val Gielgud from the Book of Wisdom, and the second from the Revelations read by His Honor Judge Gordon Clark (Cyril Hare). The service ended with the singing of Abelard's "O quanta qualia," which she had learned to love so long ago at Oxford under the baton of Dr. Hugh Allen.

Dorothy L. Sayers was sixty-four when she died, but looked years older. She had burnt herself out like a box of fireworks into which a spark has been dropped. During the course of her life she had set off rockets, Roman candles and sparklers in all directions. She had intensely loved one or two men, been loyal to all her friends, and done such work as came to her hand as well as she possibly could. She had re-aroused interest in religion at a time when people were in need of a faith of some kind. Her love of language had rubbed off on many, and above all perhaps, she had brought amusement and fun into the lives of millions. Lord Peter Wimsey refuses to die, and every few years another generation discovers him. It is the latest admirers who feel most strongly that fifty years is too long to wait to know more about his creator, and it is for them that this biography of Dorothy L. Sayers has been written.

The Works of Dorothy L. Sayers

Op 1 (verse). Blackwell, 1916.
Catholic Tales and Christian Songs (verse). Blackwell, 1919.
Whose Body? Ernest Benn, 1923.
Clouds of Witness. Ernest Benn, 1926.
Unnatural Death. Ernest Benn, 1927.
The Unpleasantness at the Bellona Club. Gollancz, 1928.
Lord Peter Views the Body. Gollancz, 1928.
Tristan of Brittany. Ernest Benn, 1929.
The Documents in the Case (with Robert Eustace). Gollancz, 1930.
Ask a Policeman (with others). Arthur Barker, 1930.
Strong Poison. Gollancz, 1930.
Five Red Herrings. Gollancz, 1931.
Have His Carcase. Gollancz, 1932.
Hangman's Holiday. Gollancz, 1932.
Murder Must Advertise. Gollancz, 1933.
The Nine Tailors. Gollancz, 1934.
Gaudy Night. Gollancz, 1935.
Busman's Honeymoon. Gollancz, 1938.
Double Death (with others). Gollancz, 1939.
Begin Here (a war-time essay). Gollancz, 1940.
The Mind of the Maker. Methuen, 1942.
The Man Born to Be King (radio cycle play). Gollancz, 1943.
Even the Parrot. Methuen, 1944.
Unpopular Opinions (essays). Gollancz, 1946.
The Heart of Stone. The Four Canzoni of the "Pietra" Group of Dante. Privately printed, 1946.
Four Sacred Plays: The Devil to Pay; The Just Vengeance; He That Should Come; The Zeal of Thy House. Gollancz, 1948.

The Divine Comedy (translation) Penguin: **Hell,** 1949. **Purgatory,** 1955. **Paradise** (with Barbara Reynolds), 1962.

The Greatest Drama Ever Staged. St. Hugh's Press, 1950.

The Emperor Constantine (play). Gollancz, 1951.

Introductory Papers on Dante. Methuen, 1954.

Further Papers on Dante. Methuen, 1957.

The Song of Roland. Penguin, 1957.

The Days of Christ's Coming (nativity story for children). Harper & Brothers, N.Y., 1960.

The Poetry of Search and the Poetry of Statement (posthumous essays). Gollancz, 1963.

The first three Wimsey books *(Whose Body?, Clouds of Witness* and *Unnatural Death)* were originally published by Ernest Benn. The rest were published by Gollancz, who eventually took over Benn's contracts. These books are all in print in hardback from Gollancz, and all the Wimsey stories are available in paperback from New English Library.

In the U.S.A. Harcourt Brace Jovanovich, Inc. published most of Dorothy L. Sayers's works (some with alternative titles) until 1954, when Harper & Row (then Harper & Brothers) purchased the plates to all of the titles except *The Nine Tailors,* and re-issued the books in the following years:

Whose Body?	1956
Clouds of Witness	1956
Unnatural Death	1956
The Unpleasantness at the Bellona Club	1957
Strong Poison	1958
The Five Red Herrings	1958
Have His Carcase	1959
Murder Must Advertise	1959
Gaudy Night	1960
Busman's Honeymoon	1960

They are all in print in the Harper edition.

Avon Books has re-issued in paperback all of the Wimsey novels except *The Nine Tailors,* and also *The Documents in the Case, In the Teeth of the Evidence, Lord Peter Views the Body* and *Hangman's*

Holiday. A collection of all the Wimsey short stories, *Lord Peter,* appeared in 1972, published by Harper & Row in hardcover and Avon Books in paperback.

The B.B.C. adapted for television four of the Wimsey novels, *Clouds of Witness, The Unpleasantness at the Bellona Club, Murder Must Advertise* and *The Nine Tailors,* and the programs were televised in the U.S.A., starting in October 1973, as part of the Public Broadcasting System's *Masterpiece Theater Series.*

This is by no means a complete list of Dorothy L. Sayers's works. Many have been translated into foreign languages, and there have been so many different editions of the Wimsey books that it is almost impossible to keep track of them. Gollancz alone have brought them out in several different ways. Equally, many of her essays have been published both separately and in collected editions.

A slight comedy, *Love All,* was produced in a small theater in 1940, but I have been unable to find a copy of this, or a record of the actual theater where it was produced; but it is believed to have been at The Torch just off Hyde Park Corner in London.